Hunter Davies is the author of forty books, including the only authorised biography of The Beatles. As a journalist, he currently writes a column about money in the *Sunday Times* and about football in the *New Statesman*. He is married to the novelist and biographer Margaret Forster and they divide their time between London and Loweswater.

RELATIVE STRANGERS

On 18 May 1932, Kate Hodder gave birth to a baby girl at Birchfield House Infirmary near Sevenoaks in Kent. Three and a half hours later, a baby boy was born. And then, forty minutes on, a second girl was delivered. But the joy at the birth of triplets — a very rare event in the 1930s — was to prove short-lived. Kate died the following day. Her husband Wills was soon struggling to cope with their six previous children, so the decision was made to offer the triplets up for adoption. Remarkably, aged sixty-nine, the three triplets were reunited. Here, their astonishing story charts their three different upbringings, and the struggles and detective work that brought them back together.

HUNTER DAVIES

RELATIVE STRANGERS

A HISTORY OF ADOPTION

AND A TALE OF TRIPLETS

Complete and Unabridged

CHARNWOOD
Leicester

First published in Great Britain in 2003 by
Time Warner Books UK
London

First Charnwood Edition
published 2004
by arrangement with
Time Warner Books UK
London

Davies, Hunter, *1936* –
  Relative strangers: a history of adoption and a tale
  of triplets.—Large print ed.—
  Charnwood library series
  1. Hodder (Family) 2. NORCAP 3. Barnardo's
  4. Adoptees—Great Britain—Family relationships
  5. Triplets—Great Britain—Family relationships
  6. Adoption—Great Britain—Law and legislation
  7. Large type books
  I. Title
  362.8′298′0941

  ISBN 1–84395–426–5

Published by
F. A. Thorpe (Publishing)
Anstey, Leicestershire

Set by Words & Graphics Ltd.
Anstey, Leicestershire
Printed and bound in Great Britain by
T. J. International Ltd., Padstow, Cornwall

This book is printed on acid-free paper

Contents

APPENDICES

Introduction

This is a book about triplets born in 1932, who were adopted as tiny babies by different parents from different social classes in different parts of the country. They were separated from one another for sixty-nine years, until they were finally reunited in 2001.

It's also a detective story — about the clues and the trails, the reasons and motives that led to two of them meeting, and how contact was eventually made with the third triplet. This final search culminated in an historic court case, which of course all the best detective stories should include.

But perhaps most importantly this is a book about adoption. Adoption is a vital part of our social history. Its own history reflects our society's ever-changing moral and social attitudes; our shifting legal and economic stances. The story of adoption reminds us of stigmas long gone. Its history takes in the nineteenth-century work of Dr Barnardo, whose homes, as you will see, have a role in our story; and the work of a modern adoption organisation, NORCAP (the National Organisation for the Reunion of Children and Parents), whose founder Pam Hodgkins — herself adopted — was the major player in the 2001 High Court case that finally brought all three triplets together.

During the last year, I have read dozens of books on adoption to understand the main elements and stages in its development; to set the triplets' history in context. I quickly discovered that it is a huge, extremely complicated, technical subject, yet I could find no one book that recounted its history from the beginning to the present day. Many of them were very academic or specialist: collections of case histories, guidelines to adoption practices, advice for people about to adopt. I was looking for a general book for the interested layman, which would help me understand how and why adoption began and how it has changed over the years. Unable to find one, and mindful of the triplets' remarkable story, I decided to attempt my own version.

When I got to grips with it, or convinced myself I had, I found the story of adoption just as fascinating as the personal stories it encompassed. Under the old systems and practices, which the triplets lived through, adoption in this country was about British babies being sent off to live with British strangers. Today that supply system has practically dried up and many adoptees come from other countries, or are older children, some of whom have developed behavioural problems that hugely affect their ability to integrate into a new, unfamiliar family. Their stories, as well as that of adoption, are constantly evolving.

Around 600,000 people who are affected by adoption remain separated from their birth families; some have not yet had the good fortune, like the triplets, to be reunited; some have chosen not to be. Adoption will continue to develop and expand, thanks to the 2002 Adoption and Children Act, which aims to increase the number of adoptions by forty per cent over the next two years. Our current prime minister has himself taken a personal interest in the subject. (Tony Blair's father was adopted and his wife Cherie has become president of Barnardo's.) No one can deny that it is an important issue.

The triplets themselves are still with us. They have had only two years together and who knows what might happen to them next. But they are alive and well and might easily go on to become the world's oldest living triplets. The extraordinary circumstances that have defined their lives make a fascinating story of our times.

Hunter Davies
Loweswater, 2003

1

The Hodder Family Hit Hard Times

William John Hodder was known by his family as Wills, which conjures up an upper-class, princely image, despite the fact that he spent his life as a farm labourer and gardener. His father and grandfather before him were also farm labourers and jobbing gardeners, each of whom rejoiced in the name of Ephraim Hodder.

Wills was born on 14 April 1896, in Stone Street, a very small, rural hamlet in the parish of St Lawrence, Seal Chart, about three miles outside Sevenoaks in Kent. In the early twentieth century there were many big estates and large fruit and hop farms in this area, lived in and worked by aristocracy, landed gentry or affluent farmers. The manual work on each was done by the labouring classes, who usually lived in cottages tied to the big estate or farm. It was only in 1934, with improvements to the railways, that Sevenoaks started to become a commuter town with locals whizzing up each day to London. In the 1920s, local workers remained in their villages and their position in life.

Wills' father Ephraim was the gardener for a big country mansion in Stone Street known as the Firs. Ephraim's house, which went with his job, consisted of two little adjoining cottages and four acres of land, and was situated opposite the main gates of the Firs.

In 1922, Ephraim's rental agreement shows that he was paying £20 a year for the property, but he could be removed on receipt of six months' notice if any 'portion of the land was needed for building or any other purpose'. Under the agreement, he undertook 'not to interfere with the Fruit Trees or the Fruit Crop which the Landlady reserves and that he will use all his reasonable care to preserve the fruit trees from injury by cattle or otherwise'.

As a young boy Wills Hodder attended the small village school beside the church. At thirteen, he joined his father on the big estate as a farm boy. Some time afterwards he started courting Kate Woolway, who was a junior maid at the Firs.

Kate came from another long-established farm-labouring family. Her father Fred was a wagoner, which was considered one step up from a carter. By tradition a carter was someone who had only a cart and horse, while a wagoner had at least two carts and two horses, plus another man to help him, usually his brother or son. In this lush heartland of Kent, with its hops and apples, plums and pears, there was always ample work for carters.

Kate was born on 26 May 1895, the oldest of five children. According to the youngest, Florrie, when she was born, sixteen years after her big sister Kate, Kate refused to come home and see the new baby. 'I think she thought it was disgraceful, our mother giving birth at her age. That's what I was told, many years later.'

At the outbreak of the First World War, when eighteen-year-old Wills joined the army, Florrie remembers how handsome he looked when he came to see Kate in his uniform. But then everybody in uniform at the outbreak of that terrible war was considered handsome and dashing, admirable and heroic.

When Florrie was about seven, she fell and cut herself one day while playing near the Firs. The lady of the house laid her out on a table in the kitchen and bandaged her forehead. While Florrie was lying there, they heard the noise of drums and then the sounds of soldiers marching down the road outside the main gate on their way to Sevenoaks. Florrie immediately jumped up from the kitchen table to look out of the window.

'Do you like soldiers, Florrie?' asked the lady of the house.

'I like my Kate's Wills,' Florrie replied.

Florrie, who is still alive, says that for many years afterwards she had to put up with endless teasing in the family for what she said that day about Wills.

Wills returned safely from the war, unlike one of his uncles, Hugh Herbert, who was killed in its last year. His name is today on the War Memorial board inside St Lawrence church, along with fifteen other parishioners who perished. His gravestone outside reads: 'Private H. H. Hodder, 273650, Labour Corps, 16 January 1918, aged forty.'

Wills and Kate got married in the church on 19 October 1919. The wedding photograph shows a large party of relations, all smart and well-dressed. Florrie, Kate's little sister, was one of the three bridesmaids. Kate herself looks like a child bride, so small and fragile. Wills is impressive in his bowler hat.

Their first home as a married couple was an old army hut, known as The Bungalow, a prefabricated wooden building which Wills helped to erect on some spare land in the village. This was where their first child, Ronald, was born, on 28 September 1920.

There exists today a family photo of Wills proudly holding baby Ron on his knee, with Wills' grandfather Ephraim and his father Ephraim beside him. The three men are sitting on kitchen chairs on what looks like a lawn or perhaps the edge of a field. It appears quite a professional photograph, in a professional pose. Did Kate, not in the photograph, take it? Ordinary folks could not afford a camera in 1920. Perhaps a travelling photographer did it, as it was a special occasion, with the birth of Wills' and Kate's first child. Four generations of Hodders in one photo — quite an achievement when you consider that the average male lifespan at the time was fifty-five and Grandpa Hodder was by then eighty-three. Baby Ron is chubby and healthy-looking, the men well-dressed, their boots highly polished. Wills and his father manage a grin, revealing a few missing teeth. They all appear happy and healthy, looking forward to a bright future.

Ron was followed by Evelyn in 1922, Kathleen in 1923, Albert (always known as Joe) in 1925,

Patricia in 1927 and Jean in 1928. Evelyn was born partially deaf and Patricia was found to be suffering from epilepsy, but even without such problems, six children in eight years was bound to take its toll: In a photograph taken after she had had the fourth of her children, Kate Hodder looks tired and thin-faced.

Around 1930 the family moved to Forge Cottage in Seal. Wills was employed on a large local farm called Hookers and towards the end of 1931 Kate found that she was pregnant for the seventh time.

She grew large very quickly, so large that as the months went on she could hardly walk. Florrie came to visit her the week before she gave birth and was amazed to see how enormous her sister had become: 'She couldn't even get out of her chair,' she recalls.

Florrie had moved to London when she was seventeen, along with her mother. Her father had died and thus they had lost their cottage. While living in Seal, Florrie had followed her sisters into service, working locally as a parlour maid. On moving to London, she had found a job working in a greengrocers. But she came back regularly to Seal to see her favourite sister.

Mrs Woolway had been up and down from London too during Kate's pregnancy to help out with the six children, for Kate was clearly not well. That week Florrie had come down with her for the day on the Sunday on a Green Line bus, but had had to get back for work, leaving her mother to stay with Kate and help with the cottage and the children while they awaited the birth. Kate and Wills had four girls and two boys so far. Would this be another boy to even things up?

Kate's six older children had been born at home without complications, but this time when the local doctor was called to examine Kate he announced he would be unwilling to perform a home delivery. From Kate's size, state of health and age — nearly thirty-seven — he could tell there might well be problems at the birth. She would be better off giving birth in a hospital.

On 18 May 1932 Kate's waters suddenly broke, some weeks before her due date. She was rushed to the nearby Birchfield House Infirmary and at 7.50 p.m. she gave birth to a baby girl who appeared normal and healthy. Kate herself, however, was in great pain. Her heartbeat was erratic, she was dangerously weak. And it now became apparent that her labour was far from over: there was another baby in her womb.

It took almost four hours of agonising struggle, sweat and tears, before a boy emerged at 11.10 p.m. But, staggeringly, this was not the end. To everyone's astonishment, half an hour later another baby was delivered — a girl. Kate had given birth to triplets. No one had suspected for a moment she might be carrying more than one child.

Even nowadays, with the use of fertility treatments, triplets are very rare: in 1990 only 201 sets were born in England and Wales. In the 1930s all multiple births were, of course, conceived naturally, and to give birth to triplets occurred only once in 10,000 births. Not only this, but the chance of any multiple-birth baby surviving at that time was just ten per cent. That all three Hodder triplets were born alive was thus little short of miraculous.

Their births were spread over four hours — an indication they were not identical. Their weights, alas, have not been recorded. The first girl was named Florence, after Kate's sister. The boy was called John William and the final girl was called May, after the month in which she was born.

Two days later Florrie, aunt to the new triplets, was awakened by the knock of a policeman at the front door. She had no phone, so a message had arrived via the local police station to say that she should return home to Seal urgently. Florrie immediately assumed that her mother must be ill. Having to look after six noisy children and care for a heavily pregnant daughter must have tired her out more than she expected.

'When I got to Stone Street, I met one of my cousins not far from the house. I asked her how mother was. She told me that mother was fine, but that my sister Kate had died. What a shock I got.'

Kate had passed away the day after the birth of her triplets. Her death certificate gives three causes of death: acute dilation of the stomach; heart failure; parturition with triplets.

'Parturition' is simply another term for giving birth. But what a shattering, horrifying parturition Kate's had been. It was a minor miracle to have given birth to three living, breathing

CERTIFIED COPY OF AN ENTRY OF BIRTH

The summary fee for this certificate is 3s. 9d.
Where a search is necessary to find the entry,
1 search fee is payable in addition.

GIVEN AT THE GENERAL REGISTER OFFICE,
SOMERSET HOUSE, LONDON.

Application Number. 449409

REGISTRATION DISTRICT.   SEVENOAKS

1932   BIRTH in the Sub-district of   Sevenoaks   in the   County of Kent

Columns:—									
No.	When and where born	Name, if any	Sex	Name, and surname of father	Name, surname, and maiden surname of mother	Occupation of father	Signature, description, and residence of informant	When registered	Signature of registrar	Name entered after registration
1	2	3	4	5	6	7		9	10*
499	Eighteenth May 1932 7.50.p.m. Birchfield House Infirmary Sundridge R.D.	Florence	Girl	William John Hodder	Kate Hodder formerly Woolgar	Gardener (Domestic) 2 Forge Cottage Seal Chart Seal Sevenoaks R.D.	W.J.Hodder Father Forge Cottage Seal Chart Seal	Twentyfirst May 1932	R.E.Milton Registrar	Adopted John Hodd.. Superintendent Registrar

*See note overleaf.

CERTIFIED to be a true copy of an entry in the certified copy of a Register of Births in the District above mentioned.
Given at the GENERAL REGISTER OFFICE, SOMERSET HOUSE, LONDON, under the Seal of the said Office, the   15th   day of   June   19 61.

This certificate is issued in pursuance of the Births and Deaths Registration Act, 1953 (1 & 2 Eliz. 2, c. 20).
Section 34 provides that any certified copy of an entry purporting to be sealed or stamped with the seal of the General Register Office shall be received as evidence of the birth or death to which it relates without any further or other proof of the entry, and no certified copy purporting to be given in the said Office shall be of any force or effect unless it is sealed or stamped as aforesaid.
CAUTION.—Any person who (1) falsifies any of the particulars on this certificate, or (2) uses a falsified certificate as true, knowing it to be false, is liable to prosecution.

BC 249749

REGISTRATION DISTRICT

1932   BIRTH in the Sub-district of _____

Columns:—	1	2	3	4
No.	When and where born	Name, if any	Sex	Name, and surname of father
500	Eighteenth May 1932 11.10.p.m. Birchfield House Infirmary Sundridge R.D.	John William	Boy	William John Hodder

CERTIFIED to be a true copy of an entry in the certified copy of a E

Given at the GENERAL REGISTER OFFICE, SOMERSET HOUSE, LONDON, ʋ

triplets, but at what a price. Her poor, battered body would appear to have been torn apart over the four hours of the delivery — until finally her heart gave out.

Her death certificate names her place of death as Birchfield House Infirmary, Sundridge, the triplets' birthplace. There is no such infirmary today, though the handsome three-storey house still stands.

Birchfield House was in fact in 1932 the local

CERTIFIED COPY OF AN ENTRY OF BIRTH

REGISTRATION DISTRICT

1932. **BIRTH in the Sub-district of**

Columns:—	1	2	3	4
No.	When and where born	Name, if any	Sex	Name, and surname of father
1	Eighteenth May 1932 11.45.p.m. Birchfield House Infirmary Sundridge R.D.	May	Girl	William John Hodder

CERTIFIED to be a true copy of an entry in the certified copy of a R

Given at the GENERAL REGISTER OFFICE, SOMERSET HOUSE, LONDON, un

workhouse. It was built in 1845 by the Poor Law commissioners at Ide Hill in the parish of Sundridge on land called Birchfield Wood, owned by the Earl of Amherst. An infirmary was later added and in the 1930s it contained 150 females. Babies were regularly born within the workhouse walls. There was also a casual ward for 'gentlemen of the road' or male vagrants, around twenty of whom would turn up most evenings and be searched, stripped and cleaned.

10

HC 790091

CERTIFIED COPY of an **ENTRY OF DEATH**
Pursuant to the Births and **Deaths Registration Act 1953**

Registration District Sevenoaks

1932 . Death in the Sub-district of Sevenoaks in the County of Kent

No.	When and where died	Name and surname	Sex	Age	Occupation	Cause of death	Signature, description, and residence of informant	When registered	Signature of registrar
Columns:	1	2	3	4	5	6	7	8	9
46	Nineteenth May 1932 Birchfield House Infirmary Sundridge R.D.	Kate HODDER	Female	37 Years	of Forge Cottage Seal chart Seal Sevenoaks R.D. wife of William John HODDER a Gardener (domestic)	Acute dilation of the stomach. Heart failure. Parturition with Triplets Certified by Arthur H. Neve Coroner for Kent after Post Mortem without inquest	William J Hodder Widower of deceased Forge Cottage Seal chart Seal	Twenty first May 1932	R. E. Milton Registrar.

Certified to be a true copy of an entry in a register in my custody.

Angela Bassards _____ Superintendent Registrar

17th September 2001 Date

Like many workhouses, it was known as 'the spike' by its regular customers and local people. Birchfield had a reputation in its day for its roughness and brutality. George Orwell refers to it in his book *Down and Out in Paris and London*, which was published in 1933 — the year after the triplets were born: 'I was warned to steer clear of Billericay and Chelmsford and also Ide Hill in Kent . . . said to be the worst spike in England.'

Once the doctor had refused to deliver poor Kate Hodder in her own home, when her waters broke she was forced to go for help to the only hospital that would take her in without charging her — the dreaded spike, some three miles away. Who knows how she got there. Perhaps a wagoner drove her in his horse and cart, a journey and a mode of transport that

Birchfield House, the workhouse where the triplets were born and their mother died

cannot have helped her condition or her chances of a safe delivery.

Wills Hodder, the 'gardener (domestic)', as he is described on the birth certificates of his triplets, was thus left a widower aged thirty-six, with nine children under the age of twelve to look after as best he could.

The triplets remained in hospital. One of them, John, was suffering from enteritis and was clearly very ill. The other two were also weak and sickly. None was expected to live.

Wills' other six children were not too healthy either. Evelyn had her ear problem and severe headaches, while Pat was still suffering from regular epileptic fits. How was Wills going to manage to care for them, on his own? Could he possibly afford to pay for help when he was a poorly paid domestic gardener? Would his family be able to assist? His mother Agnes was seventy-two — too old to be expected to lend much support. His mother-in-law was a little younger, but she was not in good health, and anyway she now lived in Harrow.

Ronald, the oldest of Wills' first six, was by now eleven and a half, so might soon be able to go out to work and bring in some money. If Wills could only maintain his health and strength and remain in work for the next year or two, he might just about manage to keep some, if not all, of his six older children at home; prevent them from being taken away from him, and into care. But the triplets seemed doomed to remain in the infirmary where they had been born. If, of course, they lived.

The 1930s was a time of widespread poverty and economic depression, with over two million out of work, but May in Kent meant blossom in the garden of England and lots of work on the big stately homes and fruit farms for the likes of Wills. Wills managed to secure a housekeeper, surprising considering his lack of money — he was earning just £2 a week — and all the mouths to feed. Unsurprisingly, with so many children to be looked after, she didn't last long. He found another, but she too quickly departed. A third housekeeper also packed it in. Yet somehow he was able to struggle on for eighteen months after Kate's death.

Things started to go wrong in January 1934. Pat, now aged seven, had a particularly serious sequence of epileptic fits and had to go into hospital. A week or so later, Wills had an accident at work. He fell and injured his knee. He had to stay at home in bed, unable to care properly for his children. There was no housekeeper to look after them so for a whole week they were left to run wild. There was naturally much tut-tutting in the local commu-nity about this disgraceful state of affairs, about the Hodder children being neglected, ill-fed, dirty, noisy, in all sorts of physical and moral danger to themselves and, very possibly, to the whole community.

In a small, rural community everyone soon finds out other people's business. Then someone usually takes it upon his- or herself to investigate; to report on what's happening; perhaps to sort things out, or to get others to do so.

In the case of Wills and his six wayward children, a Mrs Poland set in motion a series of events which led to an investigation. All these years later, Patricia remembers her as a member of a local, landed family: 'Mrs Poland was definitely gentry,' she says. 'She didn't do anything. Gentry don't do anything, do they?'

The upshot was that an officer from Dr Barnardo's called on Wills, an inspection was made and a detailed report on his situation was written up.

In the Barnardo's report, William John Hodder was described as a thirty-eight-year-old widower, a handyman earning £2 a week, of good character. His rent at Forge Cottage was 7/6 a week. He was said to be in good health but at present disabled. Kate was reported as having died of heart failure and, due to what must have been a clerical error, was given the names Edith Patricia.

When the inspector called, he found six children living with Wills. One was 'subject to fits'; all, according to the report, 'were in a dirty and neglected condition, ill-clad and poorly shod. The kitchen and the three bedrooms were in a state of disorder and there was a lack of means and utensils. The children were suffering from impetigo and were noisy.'

Mrs Poland was not simply a well-off busybody. The report says she was proposing to send the father away for a few weeks' rest and on his return to employ him as a handyman, which was kind and compassionate.

But what was going to happen to his children? The report says that the father hoped to leave

Forge Cottage and move in with his parents 'if provisions can be made for some of [them]'. It was decided that Wills' two younger girls — Patricia, aged six, and Jean, aged five, would move in with their grandparents at Stone Street, where they would eventually be joined by their father, after his rest and recuperation.

Dr Barnardo's then offered admission to the older four Hodder children. They were taken into their care on 31 January 1934. Ronald was thirteen years old, Evelyn eleven, Kathleen ten and Albert eight.

It was uncertain whether the arrangement would last for just one year, or for the remainder of their childhood: Wills had signed an agreement for twelve months, after which the case would be reconsidered. But for the moment his children had been rescued from dirt and neglect and disorder, and their immediate future was taken care of.

★　★　★

In the context of the long history of child deprivation, this was not a tragic or an unusual case. The Hodder children had not been abused, suffered cruelty or torture. In the report there is no mention of starvation or hunger, despite a 'lack of means and utensils'. Nonetheless they were lacking a mother, and currently had a disabled father with no income. But, it could have been much worse. The Hodders had escaped being sent to a workhouse — the good Dr Barnardo was looking after them.

16

RONALD JAMES, EVELYN EMILY, KATHLEEN IRENE & ALBERT LESLIE HODDER

Admitted—31st January, 1934.

RONALD	Age—13 years, 4 mos.	Born—28th Sept. 1920, at Seal Chart.		
EVELYN	„ 11 years, 7 mos.	„ 3rd June, 1922, at Fawke Common.		
KATHLEEN	10 years, 1 month.	„ 28th Dec. 1923, at do.		
ALBERT	8 years, 6 mos.	„ 9th July, 1925, at do.		

all nr. Sevenoaks.

Both parents—Church of England.

If Baptised--Yes.

Agreements for twelve months—signed by father.

Father—William John Hodder (38), handy-man, £2 p.w.; health good, but at present disabled; character good; rent 7/6 p w , Forge Cottage, Seal Chart, Sevenoaks, but address on agreements same as mat. grandparents, Blakes Green, Stone Street, nr. Sevenoaks.

Mother—Edith Patricia Hodder, died from acute dilation of stomach, and heart failure following birth of triplets, 19/5/32, in Sevenoaks P.A.C. Institution.

Application by Mrs. Poland, Godden Green, nr. Sevenoaks, Kent. Investigated by one of our officers.

The parents were married at Sevenoaks on 19/10/19, and they have had nine children, and of these the last three were triplets (1 year, 8 mos.), viz., Florence, who has been adopted by a Mrs. Davy, at Lynmouth: May, who is in the care of the National Adoption Society; and John, who was also in the care of the National Adoption Society, but who is now in Pembury P.A C. Institution suffering from enteritis. The mother died as stated above on 19/5/32. The father is respectable; he had earned £2 p.w. as a handy man; he had tried three housekeepers in succession and each one was a failure. A week ago he fell, injuring his knee, and he has since been at home confined to bed, suffering from synovitis, with no one to attend to him. There were at home with him these four children and the two sisters, viz., Edith, who is subject to fits, and Jean. The children were in a dirty and neglected condition, ill-clad and poorly-shod. The kitchen and three bedrooms were in a state of disorder, and there was a lack of means and utensils. The children were suffering from impetigo, and were noisy. Applicant proposes to send the father away for a few weeks rest, and on his return to employ him as a gardener and handy man. The father proposes to make his home with the pat. grandparents if provision can be made for some of the children.

Admission was offered to Ronald, Evelyn and Albert, and either Jean or Kathleen—Kathleen being chosen—the case to be reconsidered in twelve months time. The last consecutive six months were spent at Forge Cottage, Seal Chart, nr. Sevenoaks, Kent.

Relatives :—

Brother and sisters—John (1 year, 8 mos.), patient in Pembury P.A.C. Institution; Edith (6), Jean (5), normally with father, but now c/o pat. grandmother; Florence (1 year, 8 mos.), adopted by Mrs. Davy, Rock House, Lynmouth, Devon; May (1 year, 8 mos) Hodder, c/o National Adoption Society pending adoption.

Grandparents (pat.)—Ephraim Hodder (65), gardener, Agnes (74), Blakes Green, Stone Str 4, Sevenoaks.

Grandmother (mat.)—Elizabeth Woolway (65), w., 22 Dudley Gardens, Harrow.

Uncles & aunts (mat.)—Fred Woolway, baker, divorced, 2 children Flossie Woolway, daily worker, both with mat. grandmother; Jack Woolway, lorry driver m 2 childrou, St Marys Lane, Wrotham; Emily Sinden, bus caretaker 2 children, School House, Seal Chart.

The Dr Barnardo's report on the Hodder children

Provision for the triplets was to be very different. They too were soon to be taken into new homes, but not by an organisation — by new mothers and fathers. Since they had been born they had been with Wills very little, remaining instead in the infirmary where he visited them regularly as they slowly gained strength and health. Whilst their older siblings were being taken in by Dr Barnardo's, John and May were put into the care of the National Adoption Society. The third triplet, Florence, had already been adopted.

2

Adoption and Dr Barnardo

Adoption is an ancient practice. For thousands of years, it has been a solution for children whose birth mothers cannot, or will not, bring them up. Babies with no obvious means of support have been found in biblical bullrushes; abandoned in stone-age caves; dumped on medieval doorsteps; left at eighteenth-century workhouses; shoved under benches in nineteenth-century factories; farmed out by twentieth-century teenage mothers; found orphaned in twenty-first-century refugee camps.

The reasons and causes for their abandonment, or for the inability of their birth mothers or birth fathers to look after them, have changed over the centuries and varied from culture to culture. How to care for them has also varied.

Adoption functions in many primitive societies today much as it did for the ancient Egyptians, Greeks and Romans. In the ancient world an abandoned child from a destitute family was taken in by another member of the family or tribal unit, although not necessarily for ever. As the child grew up he or she might move from family to family, often maintaining contact with the birth mother — if she was still alive — perhaps even returning to live with her from

19

time to time. The family unit, big or small, became the parent.

At a wealthier level, it was common for a tribal leader, or in the case of the Romans, a leading citizen of some status and possession, to take over a child from its birth parents. This was more likely to be an older child, almost always a male, whom the leader would appoint as his heir. The child would be adopted to the extent of taking on the leader's family name, his position, his authority, and would be treated as his son. The object was to preserve succession, to continue the tribal or family line.

In such cases the birth parents were willingly giving up their child, seeing it as an honour, a gift to the leader or to their tribe, to do so. To adopt well reflected favourably on the birth parents, the child and the leader.

In medieval times in Britain, these two basic types of individual adoptions also prevailed. At the lower end of the economic scale, informal arrangements were made for the extended family, or the village, to care for and bring up a motherless child, though nothing would be written down or formally agreed. Affluent families in need of an heir or new blood would take in a promising boy and educate him in their own image.

Implicit in this form of adoption is the notion that its main purpose is to assist the person or persons doing the adopting — that their needs and desires are paramount, rather than those of the child. When a member or members of an extended family take in a child in need, the purpose is to help the poor child.

Hence we have — in simple terms — the dichotomy of adoption. Whose needs should matter most: the adopter's or the adoptee's? Such a question has been asked since the idea of adoption was conceived. Today it has expanded to include a third element: what about the needs of the state? What about the good of the community at large? Is it better for us all — financially and morally — if children whose natural parents are absent are in the care of the state, or in private families?

There was no clear answer to this for hundreds of years, but the medieval state did, gradually, create more structured arrangements for the care of abandoned children. Crafts and guilds created funds or systems to help the homeless offspring of their own workers, as did religious bodies and various charities. But these did not touch the chronically poor with no connections to guilds or the appropriate Churches.

From 1563 the first Poor Laws were introduced by Elizabeth I, to improve and formalise these various haphazard methods of dealing with poverty. Parishes became responsible for their own destitute, homeless, abandoned or orphaned children. Each parish imposed a Poor Law rate on its rate payers, which was decided by the local designated Poor Law guardians, who were responsible for building the local workhouses and appointing their governors. The Poor Law rate was an altruistic, democratic idea in theory, but in practice most parishes tried to keep it as low as possible, and only provided the most basic food and water and the cheapest accommodation. Poor Law guardians did not want their parish to be known as caring and generous, since they did not want to be inundated with people seeking sanctuary. So they kept their purse strings tight, and their treatment brutal.

The result was that those in most need were deterred from claiming Poor Relief, and were thus punished for being poor just as they had been before the introduction of such laws. Indeed many 'God-fearing', 'hard-working' people did consider poverty a form of crime. As for mothers giving birth out of wedlock, or abandoning their babies, they were seen as especially immoral and were also treated as criminals. A single mother had no rights, and would inevitably end up in a workhouse. There her children would be separated from her, often for good.

During the Industrial Revolution of the nineteenth century, when millions moved from working the land to urban factories, such problems got far worse. Extended family structures which had supported their own homeless, motherless children, broke down, as rural communities were splintered. Urban waifs and strays became commonplace: children who had been abandoned could no longer depend on a close-knit community or extended family to take them on, and often preferred the streets or railway arches to the workhouse.

But as these problems arose and multiplied, so

did certain solutions and saviours. For the nineteenth century was also a time of great religious fervour. Missions and Churches, at home and abroad, competed to save the souls of the poor and dispossessed; to care for and house the poor; and especially to save parentless children. One of the earliest of such saviours was Thomas Coram, a former sea captain. He was shocked by the number of abandoned illegitimate babies, born mainly to prostitutes, whom he saw on the streets of London, and in 1746 he set up what became England's first incorporated charity when he opened the Thomas Coram Foundling Hospital in central London, near the area now known as Coram's Fields. His aim was to 'protect mothers from ill-repute as much as provide for their children'. Not quite as child-centred a venture as we would expect today, but with similar aims and focus.

But, of course, the greatest and best-known saviour of nineteenth-century children was Dr Barnardo. Thomas Barnardo was born in Dublin on 4 July 1845. His father, a furrier who had originally come from Prussia, is thought to have been Jewish, his mother was an Irish Catholic. Thomas was his parents' last child. He was small and delicate as a young boy and didn't go to school until he was ten. He then progressed to a Catholic grammar school which he didn't care for. Being small, useless at sports and a self-confessed agnostic with a confusing foreign background, he got picked on and bullied. He left school as soon as he could — at sixteen — and was apprenticed to a wine merchant.

Aged seventeen Thomas underwent a religious conversion when he heard a visiting preacher call for the congregation, of which Thomas was one, to repent and devote their life to the service of God. Thomas came forward and from then on was a fervent Evangelical. He joined the Plymouth Brethren and shortly afterwards became convinced that God's purpose for him was to be a medical missionary in China. He had no medical qualifications, nor had he passed any public examinations, so in 1866, aged twenty-one, he came to London, took lodgings in Stepney and determined to get the requisite training.

He got some teaching work in a ragged school, but spent most of his time preaching — exhorting others to see the light. On his wanderings around the East End, he heard the founder of the Salvation Army, William Booth, preach, and was impressed and further inspired by his use of military uniforms and slogans offering 'soup and salvation to the poor'.

Studying medical books at night he managed somehow to get himself accepted as a student at the London Hospital. He remained firm in his aim to become a medical missionary, but the longer he stayed in London, the more he realised that work needed to be done there to help all the children he saw abandoned in the streets.

One cold and frosty night he came across a young boy sitting by a fire in the gutter. Asked where he lived, the boy replied, 'Nowhere.'

'As we looked at the little lad whom the Lord had sent to us,' Barnardo later wrote in his book,

Night and Day, 'and noticed how ill-prepared he was to resist the vicissitudes of the weather, our heart sank as we silently reflected; if all this boy says is true, how much he must have suffered! Is it possible in this great city there are others as young as this boy, as helpless, as ill-prepared to meet the trial of cold and hunger and exposure of every kind?'

It is estimated that when Barnardo came to London there were 30,000 homeless children living in the streets. So there was lots to be done, many to be saved.

★　★　★

Barnardo opened his first boys' home in 1870 in Stepney. It housed thirty-three boys. A third had jobs and therefore could afford to pay a small lodging fee. A third were unemployed, but capable of work, if they could be trained and directed. A third were destitute and needed clothing, cleaning and feeding before work could even begin to transform them.

To raise money for his boys' home, Barnardo hit upon the idea of photographing the most unkempt and destitute of these boys, just as they had appeared when he'd first come across them on the streets. He then cleaned them up and photographed them again. These 'before and after' photographs were sold to the public, producing a small income and eliciting great sympathy for each one. He also wrote and sold a booklet about his work called 'Labours of love among our East End Arabs'. (Homeless waifs were often called street Arabs.)

Barnardo's use of the new media of photography and his manipulation of public emotions attracted attention and money and helped his first boys' home to flourish, enabling him to expand and set up others. But his most important gift was as an organiser and entrepreneur. He was not content to just house and feed the destitute, he was determined to knock them into shape, train them up, teach them to work by providing means and materials. He created workshops in all his homes, in which the boys produced things to sell, such as chopped firewood; he created Barnardo messenger boys in smart uniforms, who delivered messages and packets all over London.

In 1873 Barnardo married Syrie Elmslie, the daughter of a city businessman, who was also a keen Evangelical and had helped to run a ragged school. Barnardo managed to turn his wedding into a public-relations event for his work, insisting it took place in an East End tabernacle that could hold 6000 of his friends and supporters. One of his wedding presents, from a wealthy Evangelical solicitor, was Mossford Lodge, a large house and estate in Barkingside near Ilford in Essex.

Earlier in 1873 Barnardo had opened a home for orphan and destitute girls which was run along similar lines to the boys' homes: the girls slept in dormitories, dressed in the same clothes and were given lots of works to do. The home was run by Syrie and other Christian ladies. One night Barnardo overheard some of the girls talking in their dormitory and was appalled by 'their vile conversation'. He became convinced that by allowing homeless girls of the same age to live together in such close quarters, he was 'propagating and intensifying evil'.

So, having been given Mossford Lodge, Barnardo hit upon a completely new way of bringing up his orphan girls. He built separate cottages on the estate at Barkingside — sixty in all — complete with a village green and a church. He called this the Girls' Village Home, and it continued successfully for many years.

By 1875 Barnardo had four hundred boys and girls under his care in various homes and was receiving £25,000 a year in donations. In five years he had gone from being an unknown, impecunious medical student in the East End to a much-admired philanthropist with a growing national reputation.

Naturally enough, with success and acclaim, came sniping, bad-mouthing, gossip and innuendo from his rivals. Some of the allegations were, however, more serious than mere unpleasant rumours. Firstly Barnardo was accused of falsifying his medical qualifications. He was indeed on dangerous ground in calling himself a doctor as he had never properly qualified or graduated from medical school. His supporters defended him by saying it was a tradition in the East End for all young medical students attending the poor to be addressed as 'doctor', but the facts were indisputable.

It was also alleged he was making use of some of the money flowing into his homes for his own comfort; that he was living in style at Mossford Lodge, the site of the Girls' Village Home, as if it were his country residence.

Several Christian newspapers and pamphlets actively campaigned against him, printing various accusations of cruelty and sexual abuse in some of his homes, saying that he himself had received sexual favours from one of his followers. These same pamphlets alleged, too, that his heart-breaking photographs of pathetic waifs had been doctored; that he had deliberately dressed children in rags to make their condition look far worse than it was. A mother came forward, appalled to have seen her child appear barefoot selling newspapers in a photo under the headline, 'A little waif, six years old, taken from the streets.' The mother denied her daughter had ever gone barefoot, or had sold newspapers, claiming that though they were poor, the family was respectable.

Finally, in 1877 an arbitration court was set up to investigate such allegations. Witnesses were called to give evidence for and against Barnardo. He hired a well-known QC to defend himself and his organisation against his main critic and enemy, George Reynolds, a Baptist minister.

The arbitrators finally cleared Barnardo of the more serious charges. They judged that funds had not been appropriated; that there was no evidence of cruelty in the homes; and — the final vindication — that the Barnardo homes were 'real and valuable charities and worthy of public confidence and support'.

The only allegation that stuck concerned the

photos. The arbitrators criticised the 'use of artistic fiction to represent actual fact', which they feared could 'grow into a system of deception dangerous to the cause on behalf of which it is practised'.

The matter of Barnardo's medical qualification remained cloudy. After the arbitration he spent four months in Edinburgh and obtained a certificate from the Royal College of Surgeons. This, so he maintained, entitled him to call himself doctor, although really he should not have done so as he was never a graduate.

Despite the large costs of defending himself and the loss of income during the year or so of rumours and scandals, Barnardo now went on to even greater success. The case had received extensive national publicity, which in the end helped his cause: funds began to flow in again and expansion continued. Barnardo's homes were set up all over Britain and abroad, and by the 1880s they were admitting around 1700 children a year on a permanent basis.

There is no doubt that Barnardo was a law unto himself in his childcare practices. But this was at a time when few laws existed in relation to homeless or abandoned children — there were no government social workers, and Parliament had not yet passed an adoption act — so he made up his own policies, his own systems of care. Since he had the worthiest of intentions, there were rarely problems with his approach. But then, eleven years after he had been cleared by the arbitration court, he once again became mired in controversy, with the

29

case of eleven-year-old Harry Gossage.

In 1888 Harry's mother had sold her young son to two organ grinders she'd met over a drink in a pub. They dragged him round the streets like a pet monkey, beating him up if he didn't look suitably appealing, until eventually they abandoned him in the streets of Folkestone. Harry was picked up by the police, who put him in the workhouse. A local Church of England vicar spotted him there and appealed to Barnardo personally to take him in. Barnardo's staff tracked down his mother and asked her to sign a form, giving her consent. Barnardo might have sometimes been cavalier in his approach, but he did have his own system of forms and safeguards.

One day, a Canadian called William Norton arrived at Barnardo's office in Stepney, saying he wanted to adopt a boy. Barnardo was most impressed by the stranger's appearance and demeanour, and his letters of reference from various clerics. Five boys were brought in for Mr Norton to inspect, and he chose little Harry Gossage.

Mr Norton explained he wanted to bring Harry up as his son and heir, so he asked to be allowed to withhold his address in Canada to prevent 'begging or vicious relatives' tracking him down. Dr Barnardo agreed, and Harry was handed over. Within days, he was on a ship heading for Canada with his new father.

Some time later, Barnardo's got a letter from a Mr Newdigate, acting on behalf of Harry's mother, enclosing a ten-shilling donation, and asking for Harry to be transferred to a Catholic home, at his mother's request. Receipt of the ten bob was acknowledged, but the request to transfer Harry was ignored by Barnardo's.

Then, in 1889, legal action was threatened against the organisation, at last forcing them to reveal that Harry had left them for Canada, and his whereabouts were now unknown. It had been the custom for some time for Barnardo's to export 'surplus stock' from their homes to the colonies. It was claimed that they were going to a better life there, but there was also the fact that such a policy freed up beds in the homes, enabling them to take in more waifs, and thus increase their overall totals. Barnardo had introduced a system of consent when a child was taken in, with a special clause in the letter of general consent about the possibility of emigration. The 'Canada clause' had been sent separately to Mrs Gossage, but for some reason she had never signed it. Barnardo had therefore got himself in a most embarrassing situation.

A writ of habeus corpus on behalf of the mother was issued against Barnardo, giving him three months to produce Harry. Of course they had no idea where he was or how to find him.

The case was widely reported in the press and Barnardo was criticised by various legal bodies. In his defence, and in defiance, he called several public meetings of sympathisers, in which he demanded a change in the law, which was indeed not clear. Barnardo wanted institutions like his own to be granted legal rights as guardians. His case went to the House of Lords where Barnardo conducted his own defence which in the end was successful.

He was exonerated and the case resulted in the 1891 Custody of Children Act, mocked as the Barnardo Relief Bill. This gave institutions such as Barnardo's greater powers over the children in their care and restricted the rights of parents whose intentions could be proven to be malign. Courts were now able to refuse to return children to their parents, if there was evidence of cruelty and neglect.

★   ★   ★

Dr Barnardo, as he will always be called, died in 1905 aged sixty. He was buried at Barkingside, at the Girls' Village Home. The King and Queen sent messages of sympathy to Mrs Barnardo. *The Times* described him as 'amongst this country's greatest benefactors'. At the time of his death, there were some 8000 children in his care — 'the largest family in the world' as he always called it — and his work went on, flourishing and expanding throughout Britain and abroad, as well as at Barkingside. By the 1930s, the Girls' Village Home was thriving as never before, ready and waiting to receive some of the poor Hodder children.

3

Dr Barnardo's Takes in the Hodders

The four older Hodder children were taken in by Dr Barnardo's on 31 January 1934. The two boys, Ronald and Joe, went into what was called the Boys' Garden City, at Woodford Bridge in Essex, while the girls, Evelyn and Kath, were admitted to the Girls' Village Home, three miles away in Barkingside, on the Mossford Lodge estate where Dr Barnardo had lived and was buried.

In one of his many touching publications, *Something Attended, Something Done*, published in 1889, Dr Barnardo had written a chapter entitled 'Village Home for Orphan and Destitute Girls'. In this he talked about the background to his plans for the GVH, as it became known. He had created it to address 'the pressing problem of girl waifdom'.

He explained that the idea centred around that of a family, with a mother in charge of each cottage, immediately improving on any institution. 'The ordinary workhouse,' he wrote, 'was and is too much of an institution and too little of a home. The hapless inmates are indeed rescued from want and active criminality, but are in no real sense trained for life outside the walls. Their moral fibre is unequal to the strain of temptation.'

33

CHAPTER VII

VILLAGE HOME FOR ORPHAN AND DESTITUTE GIRLS.*

Barkingside, Ilford, Essex.

How to deal with Waif Girls—New Enlargements—Still Wanted—Origin and History—New Lines of Treatment—Barrack System Wrong—Natural rather than Artificial—Mr. John Sands' Gift—Cost and Accommodation—Daily Life in the Village—Old and New—Names of Cottages—Memorial to Earl Cairns—Memorial Cottages—The Gifts of Two Universities—Urgently Needed Additions—A Hospital Required—The Village Charter—Wanted £500—A Village Church Needed—A Large Family—Mercy's House—Fleet House—The Queen's Villa—Ilford and Canada—Girls in Service—The Village Workers—How to Visit Ilford—Expense of Cottage Training—A New Family—Village Statistics—Illustrative Cases—Letters from Ilford Girls.

THE Village Home at Ilford is recognised still, as for many years past, as being in the very forefront of all preventive Institutions which profess to deal with the difficult and pressing problems of girl waifdom. God's blessing has rested abundantly upon this branch ever since, sixteen years ago, the first half-dozen cottages were founded in a very conscious sense of the feebleness of the experiment. Speaking from the merely material point of view, it is difficult for a visitor to realize that the whole site of the Village, even so lately as 1873, was a ploughed field. Each successive year has brought a record of further enlargement, and most of the annual reports have therefore had to deal with a different number of cottages. From the very first the Ilford work has been in healthy growth. At the close of 1888, however, I am able to announce that the original plan of the Village is *practically* finished, *so far as regards its cottage homes*, though other buildings are still re-

* A large and beautiful Institution on the Family or Cottage system, consisting of forty-nine detached cottages and four larger households, forming a Village. Provides accommodation for nearly 1,100 girls, who are trained for domestic service at home or abroad, and brought up in Christian, homely ways.

All the girls at the GVH went to a school on the campus run by Barnardo's staff, until later the local LEA took it over. From the age of twelve the girls were trained for domestic service in its various branches, from cooking to seamstressing to housemaiding, preparing them for a job in the outside world.

In the 1930s, when the Hodder girls arrived there, a leaflet about the GVH appealing for funds described it as 'a rural paradise' far removed from the slums and poverty of the inner cities. By then two more village greens, several fountains, a clock tower, a laundry, a school, shops and five more separate cottages had been built, housing in all 1250 girls. A large fence surrounded the ground to keep the girls in and prowlers out.

In the leaflet, a lady visitor is quoted on an inspection at the village's own hospital. ' 'What is that doggie called?' asked a small mite, pausing between a spoonful of soup to look at the black fox fur I wore. I invented an answer without delay. 'I asked him if he wanted to come with me in the train to see you this morning.' A small hand crept out and stroked the fur. This performance was repeated at other beds . . . It is paradise to be a happy, healthy rollicking child of Barkingside Village.'

A book published in 1948 called *The Likes of Us*, by a former GVH girl Miss G. V. Holmes, tells of daily life in the GVH in the 1920s and 1930s. Each cottage had around twenty girls, with three to six to a bedroom. Everyone, of every age, had a job. A cottage usually had a feeble-minded member, who would be affectionately known as 'Potty'. A 'pug' was the nickname for a favourite or creep. There was a daily head-lice inspection, a regular mastoid ear clinic, but lots of fun and games and plenty of Bible readings.

There were no uniforms, but the girls mainly

wore gym tunics, which looked like a uniform. It was rare to get new clothes, or even new shoes. Everything was handed down or donated. In some cottages clothes were pooled. Letters were opened before you received them, which annoyed some of the older girls.

Miss Holmes clearly loved her life at the GVH. Almost all the girls and staff were kind. She was thrilled by Founder's Day, when there was a garden party for the nobs to visit in their best frocks and top hats, and she loved the annual trip to the Albert Hall, when a huge show was put on to attract funds for the homes.

The only criticism she had was of an unnamed teacher, who terrified girls by cornering them demanding to know what they thought about at night. She said this was worse than getting the cane as the woman was scary and would insist the girls talk to her until some, who had had terrible pre-Barnardo's experiences, would eventually pour out their awful nightmares. Miss Holmes conceded that the teacher might have been influenced by the fashionable psychiatric theories of the time, but there is the lingering sense that she may have been getting some kind of twisted satisfaction from such confrontations.

Despite this, Miss Holmes is full of praise for the GVH. Her only regret is that when she was older and out of the home she found that people treated her differently when they discovered she had been a Dr Barnardo's girl.

★   ★   ★

36

The Boy's Garden City came much later than the Girls' Village Home, building on its success. In 1909 Barnardo's bought an old country house in Woodford Bridge with thirty-nine acres for £6000. It was formally opened in 1912, with thirteen new houses for three hundred boys. This increased eventually to nineteen houses, which held in total 750 boys.

The idea was to remove boys from the overcrowded, old-fashioned Barnardo homes in the East End, and enable them to thrive in fresh air and open countryside. Each house was under the control of a mature woman and another female assistant. While the girls were prepared for domestic service, the boys did a lot of manual labour, such as gardening, to ready themselves for future jobs, but also to grow their own vegetables and flowers. The BGC had its own church, swimming pool and school.

In its early days, just after the First World War, the regime at the BGC was very tough and military. The boys wore sailor suits, their hair was close-cropped and they were strip-washed twice a day under the freezing-cold spray of a water-pipe. By the 1930s when the Hodders arrived, things were slightly less severe. Older boys were permitted fringes and the uniform had gone, but most wore the same style of handed-down shorts and pullovers, which looked like a uniform. Socks were worn turned down below the knee, without garters after it was discovered that they were being used for catapults.

Eighty-one-year-old Horace Miller was in the

Garden City during the 1930s at the same time as the Hodder boys. He clearly remembers the governor, a Captain Lewin, as a terrifying figure. 'At Christmas time, he wore his full naval uniform, with his sword. I can see him giving a boy six of the best in the dining room for having run away.'

Mr Miller was taught shoe-repairing while at the BGC, a job he took up when he left. He later became a security guard at the British Museum and remained there until he retired.

'I didn't like the Garden City at the time. The food was horrible — soup with potato peel floating in it, rice pudding with maggots in — but I am grateful for what they did for me. They learned me to be clean.'

Richard Avery is another Barnardo boy, but he has happier memories. In 1935, aged three, he was taken into the Girls' Village Home. This was most unusual, but both his parents had died and he had four older sisters, so an exception was made. When he left in 1946 Barnardo's got him a job in the City as an office boy, and found him digs. He retired in 2002, aged seventy, as sales director of an electrical company in Bristol.

'I was very happy [in the GVH], apart from when we got liver. Pig's liver it was. If you didn't eat it at lunch, you got it at tea. Being a boy probably helped me. I read an interview many years later in a Barnardo's magazine with the woman who'd been a house mother. She said one day a little girl came down the stairs crying, so she asked what was wrong. 'There's a little girl in the bath with a thumb sticking out of her tummy,' she said. I'm pretty sure that was me.'

★　★　★

Barnardo's still have the full records of the Hodder children. They were examined and processed at 18–26 Stepney Causeway in London's East End, which was still the headquarters of the Barnardo's homes. Their weights, heights and medical conditions were duly recorded, and show that they were all very small and light for their age. Ronald, aged thirteen, the older of the two boys, was only four feet eight inches and weighed 5.5 stone. His vision, hearing, glands, ears, mental condition were all classed as normal. He was not suffering from rickets, but his skin was scarred by impetigo and under the section marked 'deformities' he was said to have scoliosis, which is curvature of the spine.

Evelyn, aged eleven, was only four feet three inches and weighed four stone. She too had impetigo and her teeth needed treatment, but everything else appeared normal. Kath's skin was described as 'neglected', her general physique was 'poor, undernourished'. Under deformities, Kath was described as 'flat-chested, needing physical drill'. The Hodders were then sent off to their respective homes: the boys to the BGC; the girls to the GVH.

Throughout their Barnardo's lives they were each regularly weighed and checked, their progress noted. Their files also contain letters and notes written about them while in residence. Some of these are fascinating and informative, especially any correspondence involving Wills. They show clearly that he had not lost contact with his children, nor interest in their well-being and future. In June 1936, after his children had been in the home for two and a half years, Wills wrote to say that he had fixed up a possible job for Ronald, who was now coming up to sixteen. A Colonel Rogers of Riverhill, Sevenoaks, was interested in taking Ronald as a house boy, and he would be writing to confirm it. 'This place is a great opening for a lad to start in life,' wrote Wills. 'I personally think [it is] well worth consideration. I have seen Mrs Poland of Godden Green who[se] influence was used for getting my children into your homes and she considers [it] a grand offer. You will also hear from our vicar who thinks it is a splendid start in life.'

Colonel Rogers does confirm the offer in a brief handwritten note, while the vicar sends a rather pompous typed note. He says he has known the Hodder family for some years and is pleased that the elder son will be 'putting to some practical use the training he has received from your influence and instruction'. He adds a warning note: 'At the same time I feel that these young folks should be made to realise that for about the first six months they are very raw material in most respects and should understand that a sojourn of not less than two years should be their intention, unless, of course, there is any really good reason for leaving sooner.'

Barnardo's then sent an inspector to check out Colonel Rogers' house. The colonel himself was away fishing, but the inspector saw the housekeeper and was most impressed. 'Colonel and Mrs Rogers are very wealthy and their estate is magnificent, fully staffed,' he reported. He saw the room where Ronald would live, which was 'nicely furnished' and said the wage would be '£16 per annum, plus two suits of clothing'. He also went to see Wills Hodder at his house. It is clear that Barnardo's procedures were all very thorough and paid real attention to detail. Would a modern-day social worker do any better, spend any more time or money on background research, or write up a fuller report?

The result was that on 30 June 1936 Ronald left Barnardo's. The official form from the governors of the Boys' Garden City, signed by Captain Lewin, stated that Ronald Hodder 'was restored to his father for a situation'. It confirms that the boy's clothes have been returned from Stepney, where presumably Ronald was discharged, and that all his Barnardo's belongings have been taken back, except for his new blue mackintosh. Captain Lewin is most worried about this: 'Will you kindly give instructions for its return to us as soon as possible,' he writes.

So, that was Ronald, the oldest of the nine Hodders, settled out into the world.

On 1 August Ron sent a letter to the BGC: 'I have been in my situation a month and I am writing to you as requested. I am quite happy here.' He gave his hours and duties: up at 6.30 a.m. to open up the basement and see to

41

R. J. Hodder

Dear Mr Chapman,
This boy was restored to his father for a situation 30. vi. 36. His clothes have just been returned to us from Stepney, but his new thin machintosh has been kept altogether. Will you kindly give instructions for its return to us as soon as possible. Yours sincerely
Gwillian Lewin

the boiler; shoe cleaning; washing silver; a little scrubbing; help with lunch; help with dinner; polishing the shoes again; bed at 10 p.m.

A Barnardo's official replied sounding very pleased, saying he hoped Ron would qualify for one of the prizes awarded to ex-Barnardo boys and girls for each year of good service away from the home, and finishing his letter: 'When next you are writing, perhaps you would let me know how you like Sevenoaks. The surrounding countryside is very beautiful and I am sure you will find many lovely walks.'

* * *

The two Hodder girls were put into different cottages when they arrived at the Girls' Village Home.

In July 1935 Miss Mary Forbes, who now

resided at the estate where Wills Hodder worked, wrote to offer the two girls a summer holiday. 'Their grandfather has been gardener here for forty-nine years. Such a dear, dear man. The mother was a housemaid to my predecessor and married Hodder's only son. Her death after triplets (all lived and thrived) was very tragic. I always hoped this little family would grow into my staff in very old age.'

Barnardo's graciously agreed, adding that Kathleen and Evelyn were 'getting on extremely well here and are such nice, happy children'. They do point out that their travel expenses will have to be paid, which will come to 4/6 if they go by train, for which they can obtain special fares.

During 1936, internal reports stated that Kathleen was 'intelligent, willing, useful, but very small for hospital work'. But Evelyn's reports were not as good. They varied from 'very deceitful at times . . . dirty worker . . . not at all capable for her age', to 'tries hard to improve, satisfactory but rather slow'.

In June Wills wrote from Stone Street, where he was living with his parents and his remaining two children, Pat and Jean, to ask if this summer Evelyn and Kath could have their holiday with him and their grandparents, who, he added would pay their travel expenses.

Barnardo's wrote to Miss Forbes to inquire whether Mr Hodder had sufficient accommodation, asking, a trifle suspiciously, 'whether the arrangement would be quite satisfactory in every way?'

Miss Forbes' reply is not in the files, but it

must have been pretty damning. 'I am glad to have an opinion about the Hodder relations,' Barnardo's wrote to her. 'We will certainly send the two girls to a camp this year and refuse the invitation.'

Poor old Wills. He never knew what had gone on behind the scenes, he simply received the following letter on 15 June:

```
AH/BR          15th June, 1936.


Dear Sir,

        I am writing to say that I am

afraid we cannot allow Evelyn and

Kathleen to go for a holiday.

        We have already arranged for

them to go with some of their friends

for a holiday which they will very much

enjoy.

              Believe me,

                    Yours truly,


Mr. W. J. Hodder,
B lakes Green,
        Stone Street,                Governor.
            Sevenoaks,
                Kent.
```

Was there some serious reason for their refusal? The only clue in the files is a letter a couple of months later, in August 1936, from Mrs Poland. She was the woman who had first called in Barnardo's and had apparently been most supportive, sending Wills on holiday when he was ill.

She was writing to them about Ronnie, who was still a houseboy at Colonel Rogers': 'It is a splendid start for the boy to be employed there. I should suggest a close watch is kept on [him] by one of your officers as the father's influence may not be too good. He is a slacker, but I understand is in full-time work so is quite able to pay what he arranged for the three children.'

In the file this note is described as an 'extract from letter received from Mrs Poland'. So perhaps she threw in some even more critical remarks about Wills which they expurgated. As for the reference to the three children, this presumably meant the three still in Barnardo's, for whom he was probably meant to send some money.

★　★　★

When Evelyn reached fourteen in 1936, Wills tried to get her out of the Village Home, again by lining up a member of the local gentry to write and offer her a job, in this case the wife of the Stone Street vicar. However this time Barnardo's declined: 'She is much too young to go out to service. We give our girls two years' training after they leave school and do not let them go out

45

until they are sixteen years of age. I am sure you will realise that we do this for girls' own benefits and find that it is much the best plan.' In March 1937 Wills tried again to get another local woman to offer Evelyn a job. The reply was the same, only shorter. But that summer he did manage to have both of his girls home for their summer holidays. He must have had good reports this time.

In the following summer of 1938, Wills wrote to ask again if his children could have their summer holidays with him, adding that he had a suitable job lined up for Evelyn, who was now sixteen. Barnardo's agreed to this, but were concerned about Evelyn starting work: 'As I think you know, she is rather slow and backward and we feel requires further training before going out. I had hoped to try her soon in one of our hostels near here, from where the girls go into daily places. I think it would give her a better chance than going straight to sleep in a strange place. If, however, the lady about whom you write realises that Evelyn is slow and would still like her, perhaps she would write to me.'

Wills was clearly put out by this reply. 'In regards to her being backward,' he wrote, 'I think she would do better out on her own than in the homes. At least this is what I found with their brother who was at the Boys' Garden City.'

In a later letter he maintained this theme. 'Several ladies have told me it is very hard for girls or boys to shake off the [children's] home nature. Personally I think it is time Evelyn began to make a move.'

Now that Evelyn had reached the age of sixteen Barnardo's could not hold on to her much longer, so they contacted a lady who had offered her a job — Mrs Ritchie, wife of the vicar of Shoreham, Sevenoaks — making it clear to her that Evelyn Hodder 'is rather childish for her age'.

But the job worked out and on 27 July Evelyn left Barnardo's for good. She was by now four feet eleven inches and just over seven stone. Her mentality was classed as 72–74, which is not explained, but could refer to her IQ — evidence that she was slow.

Mrs Ritchie had to sign a form agreeing to various conditions, which included allowing 'the girl to attend a place of worship once on Sunday' and not permitting 'her to visit or be visited by relatives without first obtaining permission from the homes'.

This was a standard leaving form (after all, working at a vicarage, you would be expected to be allowed to attend church), so the ban on relatives visiting without permission was not aimed at Wills personally. Many of the girls and boys at Barnardo's had come from families that might exert a bad, not to say evil or cruel influence on them, so the organisation had to put such measures in place. (This dilemma still exists today, even more so now that contact is encouraged between children in care and their birth families.)

The records over the years on Kathleen cover much of the same ground, but they also include a letter from the governor in reply to one from

DR. BARNARDO'S
GIRLS' VILLAGE HOME, BARKINGSIDE.

SERVICE DEPARTMENT.

DATE	SURNAME: CHRISTIAN NAME.	BIRTH DATE AGE	COTTAGE
27. 7. 38	HODDER. Eveline.	3.6.22. 16.	Rose

I Certify that I have examined the above.................................

her condition is as follows :—

Height... 4' 11½"

Weight.... 7st 1½lbs.

Throat & Nose.... N

Ears......... N

Heart..... N.A.D.

Lungs........ N.A.D.

Spine........ N.

Feet......... N.

Vision : Right eye.... $\frac{6}{6}$

Left eye....... $\frac{6}{6}$

Mentality.... 12.7" March '37.

Pass doing Service

Signed................
Medical Officer

Date.... 2~ 7. 38

Evelyn's final report on leaving Barnardo's in 1938

Evelyn, written after a visit to her sister when she had found her very unhappy. 'After having nearly six years in the homes at Barkingside, I feel there must be something a little wrong,' she writes, and asks if she could use her influence to move Kath to Evelyn's old cottage. Five days later the governor writes back to say Kathleen has been moved. There is also a letter from Miss Forbes, who has been checking on the Hodders again. She mentions that one of the sisters at home (Pat) has fits and that the grandmother 'is a most odd and difficult person'. Perhaps it was these sorts of comments that prejudiced Barnardo's against Wills, rather than his own conduct.

Over the years, Kathleen emerged as the brightest of the Hodders, and as is often the case with bright children, she had a streak of rebellion within her. In October 1938 she appeared to have got mixed up with some naughty girls.

'Three house girls, —— , —— and Kathleen Hodder, walked out of the cottage this morning. I believe they are somewhere in the village. —— has done this before and has been very sullen since she did not have a holiday. —— is a great agitation and not a pleasant person to have in a schoolgirl cottage. Kathleen Hodder is a nice child and is learning but will not take correction.' Later that evening they were all found by a matron wandering round the village and were taken back to their cottage. Evidence, perhaps, of Kathleen's unhappiness in her cottage.

As with Evelyn, there is a sequence of letters when Kath got to sixteen and her father tried to fix her up with a job. This time he managed it quite smoothly. On 19 September Kath left Barnardo's and, like her sister, went into service in a local vicarage.

★　★　★

Thus Wills had finally got his three oldest children out of Barnardo's and into work not far from his own home. But alas, some of those warnings mentioned by Mrs Poland about Ronnie proved to be correct. In February 1937 Barnardo's sent an inspector to Colonel Rogers' home and he learnt from the housekeeper that Ronald was not giving satisfaction.

'She spoke bitterly about his being slovenly at work and also in appearance,' the inspector wrote. 'With regards to his conduct, she found him quite honest . . . but he is not suited for housework. I suggested that perhaps a job in the garden might be more suited to him, but apparently this has been tried and they find him just as stupid in this direction.'

The inspector gave Ronnie a serious talking-to and went to see Wills, whom 'the lad visits by cycle when he is off duty'. Wills appeared surprised that his boy was not doing so well, but promised to have a stiff talk with him as well. The inspector reported he was to be given another chance.

A month later Ronald got the sack. Colonel Rogers wrote to Wills saying he'd given the boy a month's notice. 'If I were you, I would put him to work outdoors and keep an eye on him,' he added. Wills told Barnardo's all this in another letter, which was very honest, saying he was looking for another situation for Ronald. Barnardo's replied by saying they would do so as well.

In the files, there are few personal details about Joe, the youngest of the four Hodders, but they state that he was 'removed by his father on 12 September 1939'. Because he was restored to his own family and not sent by Barnardo's into service, as with the other Hodders, they did not have any after-care notes about him.

He was by then aged fourteen, so Wills had managed to get him out two years earlier than Ronald, Kath or Evelyn. The date probably explains why: nine days earlier, Britain had declared war on Germany. Ronald was already in the army. National evacuation schemes for children had been put in place. Barnardo's, like the country at large, had now got other things to worry about.

4

Florence's Adoption

After the older Hodder children had gone into Barnardo's in 1934, they lost contact with the triplets. They had little memory of their three younger siblings anyway, who had been just twenty months old when they had last seen them.

By the time the four of them came out of Barnardo's, they were ready for work, or at least ready for war. They had no idea if the triplets were even alive. All they knew was that they had been adopted, somewhere, by some people, some years previously.

The internal document about their admittance held in the Barnardo archives (see page 14) and not seen by any family members until many decades later did give a clue as to the whereabouts of the triplet known at the time as Florence: 'Florence,' it said, 'has been adopted by a Mrs Davy of Lynmouth.'

This information was presumably given by Wills, but it doesn't say how and when the adoption took place. The full details will never be known, since vital documents were lost in the war, but it would appear that the triplet known as Florence, the first born, was around eight months old when she was taken away to Lynmonth.

Lynmouth is a little harbour in north Devon. Above it, on a cliff, is Lynton. Together they have a population of some 2000 and form a picturesque tourist attraction, handy for Exmoor and the Bristol Channel. Emily Davey, the woman who adopted Florence, who shall henceforth be known as Gill, as she was named by her new mother, was at the time running a guest house on the seafront at Lynmouth.

Emily Rose Moore was born in 1895. She married Percy Davey, a signwriter and decorator, in 1915. (In the family, and in the village, the marriage was talked about for many years because Emily was driven to the church in a taxi — it was the first time anyone had ever seen a taxi in Lynmouth.) Emily and Percy had two children: Pearl, born in 1916, and Raymond, born in 1923. The marriage collapsed after about ten years and they got divorced, although they still remained in touch. Emily was thus left to bring up her two children on her own, with the help of her mother. Financially, they were reasonably well off, because of the little guest house and tea garden.

In 1933, by which time Pearl was sixteen and Raymond was ten, they read in a newspaper — possibly the *Daily Mirror* — about a gardener from Sevenoaks who was looking for someone to adopt his baby triplets. I have been unable to find this cutting, but Raymond, now aged seventy-eight and still living in Devon, remembers it well:

'Mother read it first and showed it to me. It told how the mother had died after giving birth

53

to triplets and the father had been left with nine children under eleven, including the triplets. Mother said to me, 'Poor little dears, shall we have one of them?' I said, 'Oh please, please. I'd love to have a little sister.' So my mother decided to write to the *Daily Mirror* for more details. I'm sure it was the *Daily Mirror*. That was the paper we took.'

Not long afterwards a nurse came down from London to Exeter, bringing one of the triplets. Raymond and Emily went over to Exeter and on the station platform they saw Gill for the first time.

'I had chosen Gill. I don't know why. I just liked the look of her, from her photograph. I said to my mother, 'Let's have that one.' I can't remember if their photograph was in the papers or we were later sent photographs by Dr Barnardo's, or someone else, for us to see them. But I do remember looking at the photo — and it was me who picked out Gill. I used to tease her, many years later, by saying I picked her because she was a snotty-nosed little bugger.'

Raymond is clear in his memory of that day. The nurse, he says, was a large, rather terrifying-looking woman in a navy blue uniform with a flowing navy blue headdress, the kind that matrons used to wear. He presumed she was from Dr Barnardo's. 'I can see her clearly on the platform, holding baby Gill in her white bonnet.'

On the other hand it could have been a nurse working for or supplied by the National Children's Adoption Society, who had the other two triplets in their care by 1934, if not earlier,

54

waiting for someone to come along and adopt them.

Raymond and his mother took the baby back with them on the train and Gill's new life began.

It was Emily herself who officially adopted Gill. She was, of course, a single woman at the time, which was most unusual and suggests that the arrangements for the adoption were relatively informal. Gill believes some sort of papers must have been signed, but she has never seen them: 'I don't think I ever went into Dr Barnardo's or any sort of home. I think I lived at home, with my father, until I was adopted — then the other two went into a home, while they waited. And waited . . . ' This would explain why her father Wills knew what had happened to her, as can be seen on that Barnardo's admission document.

Wills Hodder visited Lynmouth a few times over the following years, which indicates he was trying to be a caring father, even from a long distance. Rock House was quite a big establishment, with eight bedrooms and a tea garden, so Emily Davey was able to put him up. On at least one occasion he brought with him Pat, one of his two girls who did not go into care. Gill has no memory of this — she was too young.

'Oh, I can remember him coming,' says Raymond. 'He was a smart-looking man with a dark moustache. It was a holiday for him, and for Pat. We knew Pat had fits, and she had them when she was with us. I was a bit frightened when it first happened, but my mother coped all right. She was a very sensible woman.'

In the family, the story goes that Wills wanted

55

to marry Emily but she wasn't keen: she couldn't face taking on another eight children. He did propose, but she turned him down and later married someone else. After that, naturally enough, Wills stopped visiting.

'I was never told any of this until very much later,' says Gill. 'But I have a clear memory of my mother parcelling up presents every Christmas, which she said were going to four special children in Dr Barnardo's. I never knew who they were, that they were my brothers and sisters, but I always thought it was a nice thing to do.'

In the summer of 1935 or 1936 Florrie, Kate Hodder's younger sister, also made a visit to Devon.

'I had Gill's new address and I knew that was her new name. I found the house and one day I went and looked over the wall and saw her playing. I was sure it was her. We'd always wondered what had happened to her. But I didn't approach her or tell anyone who I was. I just watched. You didn't, did you? You wasn't allowed. Adoption was secret in those days. You were not supposed to make contact, ever again.'

Florrie made the trip only once, but it satisfied her that Gill was being well looked after and had acquired a happy new home.

★　★　★

While Gill was growing up she never knew she was adopted. Her mother never told her. Even more surprising, Raymond never let it slip out.

She accepted that Gillian Florence Davey, as she became, had always been her name. Looking back, she presumes it was changed by deed poll, but again, those papers have gone missing.

She was fortunate, entering a fairly well-off, contented family — even if it had no father figure at first — in a small established community. All her early childhood memories are happy ones — playing with Raymond, collecting winkles on the beach. They always got on very well, and still do — they are certainly as close and loving as a real brother and sister.

Gill was sent to a little local private school, Henwick Preparatory (the guest-house business must have been doing pretty well), which she loved. She was average at English and Maths but liked the arts and crafts and was always top in needlework.

Gill first discovered she was adopted at school, aged thirteen: 'A girl in my class, Gillian Briggs, told me in the playground one day. I don't know what we were talking about, whether we'd had a row or not, but she suddenly said to me, 'You haven't got a mother and father — you're adopted.' I said, 'No, I'm not.' She said, 'Yes, you are.' I didn't know, of course, what adopted meant. When I got home, I asked my mother. She said it was true. I was adopted. She told me the story [of] her and Raymond going to the station in Exeter and picking me up. She said I was picked out because I was special.'

It was around this time that Emily revealed that the parcels to Dr Barnardo's had been for Gill's brothers and sisters. 'From then on, I knew

I was adopted — and I was also told that I was a triplet. But that's all I ever knew. I never asked any more. I just accepted it. It didn't bother me or worry me, either way. As far as I can remember.

'Well, perhaps it did bother me, a little bit. There was a period, now I think about it — I don't know when, but some time after I learned I was adopted — when if I was cross, or had been told off, I would put my arms round my dog Micky and say 'Let's run away Micky, and find our own people.'

'I would never have done so, of course. I was just saying it, in a bad mood or whatever. I did have such a very happy childhood. I loved my mother and Raymond. They were always kind to me. I do honestly think being adopted never seriously worried me. I have no memory of lying awake, wondering about it. I just accepted what I had been told. I didn't ask any more. I suppose I quite liked the idea of being special.'

Some months later, in 1946, Emily remarried and became Mrs Richard Rodd. He was a local man and had been one of Emily's boyfriends when they were younger.

'Raymond and I didn't know it was happening. They just went off one lunchtime on their own to Barnstaple and got married in the register office. Then they came back and told us.' Gill therefore had a third change of name, becoming Gillian Rodd by deed poll.

During the war, while her older brothers and sisters, who were, of course, still unknown to her, did their war work, Gill helped out her mother. Lynmouth became very busy as all the local guest houses filled up with evacuees.

'They were mostly families from London, young children with their mothers and aunts. There were no men. They were away fighting. I quite enjoyed it. It was good fun, having the house filled all the year round with children of my age.

'We didn't get bombed in rural Devon, of course, but there was one German plane which got shot down locally. I think he'd got lost over Exmoor when he should have been heading to bomb the docks at Plymouth. When we heard he'd been shot down, my big sister Pearl was in hospital about to give birth to her first baby. She said, 'Oh, I hope that Jerry doesn't end up in this hospital with me.' And that was exactly what happened.

'During the war in Lynmouth I used to go at night and sit on the sea wall and watch the lights of the raids on Swansea, over the Bristol Channel. You could see it all clearly. We had barrage balloons locally, in case anything came our way. One of them got free and flew away and landed in our tea garden at Rock House. Everyone was told not to smoke a cigarette anywhere near it, in case it blew up.

'One day I was with a woman who was living in Lynmouth at the time and we were watching a convoy of boats going up the Bristol Channel. She told me her son was on one of the boats and she was so worried about him. She was moving up and down the Bristol Channel, staying in guest houses, to keep an eye on him.

'As we were watching the boats that day, there was a massive explosion. I think a German submarine had been lying in wait. Anyway, this boat was blown up and her son was killed in front of her eyes. It was such a horrible sight, watching it blow up, thinking of all the people on board.'

In 1946, aged fourteen, Gill left school to work full-time with her mother and step-father in the family guest house. In some ways you could say that at fourteen she had ended up with no better a job, or any more qualifications than her brothers and sisters, the ex-Barnardo ones who had gone into service. But she'd had a very secure happy childhood as part of a loving family. She had not had to wear hand-me-down clothes, or eat up her liver.

5

May's Adoption

May was the next triplet to be adopted. Her certificate of adoption survived, though it was many decades before it was found by the other triplets.

May was adopted, aptly enough, in May 1934, aged two. From then on she became known as Helena Mary. On paper her adoption could not have been more suitable, more propitious, more fortunate. Many adoptees, then and now, are taken in by a better-off, more stable family of a higher social class, who can provide many of the advantages that the birth family, for whatever reasons, are unable to provide. Admittedly the unwanted child of a middle-class young girl is not certain to be taken in by an equally middle-class family, but as a rule adopted children usually go up on the social scale.

Gill's family was fairly well off, but she was sent to a single mother. Socially, she had risen several notches — a guest-house owner is generally seen as of greater status than a jobbing gardener — but she was still moving into an essentially working-class home, where the norm was to leave school at fourteen and get a job.

Helena, however, was adopted into a family with two happily married, middle-class parents,

61

CERTIFIED COPY of an Entry in the ADOPTED CHILDREN REGISTER

(16 & 17 Geo. V., cap. 29).

Given at the GENERAL REGISTER OFFICE, SOMERSET HOUSE, LONDON.

Application Number A.C.R.17593

No. of Entry.	Date of Entry.	Name of Adopted Child.	Sex of Adopted Child.	Name and Surname, Address and Occupation of Adopter or Adopters.	Date of Birth of Child (see Footnote).	Date of Adoption Order and Description of Court by which made.	Signature of Officer deputed by Registrar General to attest the Entry.
28927	Ninth May 1934	Helena Mary	Female	Russell Eric Thomas The Manse 25 Ravenscroft Park Barnet, County of Hertfordshire Jennie Thomas (wife of above)	Eighteenth May 1932	First May 1934 The County Court Barnet	Chas. M. Watts

CERTIFIED to be a True Copy of an Entry in the Adopted Children Register maintained at the General Register Office.

Given at the GENERAL REGISTER OFFICE, SOMERSET HOUSE, LONDON, under the Seal of the said Office, the 18th day of May 1934.

A 4425

one of whom was a public-school-, Oxbridge-educated professional. They might not have been hugely wealthy, but they must have been considered highly desirable when they first approached the National Children's Adoption Society looking for a little girl.

Helena was not just moving upmarket but, unlike Gill in her remote rural community, she was going from the country to a city. Helena's adoption order was issued on 1 May 1934 at the county court in Barnet, north London. The address of her new parents, as stated on her adoption certificate, gives an immediate clue to the profession of her new father — The Manse, 25 Ravenscroft Park, Barnet. She had been adopted by a clergyman, the Reverend Russell Eric Thomas, and his wife, Jeanie Thomas.

Eric, as he was always known, was a tall, slim, rather dashing Congregational minister. He was born in Harrogate in 1889 to a father and grandfather who were also Congregational ministers. He went to Cambridge University, was ordained and took up his first pastorate in Essex. During the First World War he saw service in Egypt, Gallipoli and India. He was an active soldier, later becoming an army chaplain.

Helena remembers him talking about his wartime experiences — how he had fought alongside some New Zealand soldiers who became close friends, but all of whom died. He also used to tell her about his time in Mesopotamia, which was not as dramatic or dangerous, mainly consisting of looking after the regimental animals. 'He always said he never wanted to see a donkey again in his life.'

After the First World War he returned to Essex and in 1921 married Jean Laing, whose family were also devoted Congregationalists. Jeannie, as she was always called, had gone to college herself and become an art teacher. It was said in the family that she had collared Reverend Thomas in the vestry one day and asked him to marry her.

They moved to various churches around the country, including St George's Congregational church in Middlesbrough. While there, having been married for some ten years without having had any children, they decided to adopt a little girl, whom they called Pamela. She was born in Scotland and adopted by the Thomases from a home or through a church agency in Edinburgh. Specific details are not known, but Pamela herself is clear about the exact day she was adopted — 21 August 1930.

The family moved to Barnet and four years later Eric and Jean decided to adopt another girl, a baby sister for Pam.

Both Pam and Helena recall their mother as being ill a lot of the time, but all their memories of their father are rosy. He delighted in singing with them — he had perfect pitch — and reading to them.

'Every evening after tea he read us a story,' says Helena. 'There was one book he used to read that had 365 tales in it. I can remember one about Turnip Top. He played cards with us, and our mother did as well — rummy and whist and snap — and he listened to *Children's Hour* on the radio with us.'

Reverend Thomas does sound a remarkable man, well known and admired in Congregational circles of the time, an energetic, muscular Christian who devoted his life to God but was also in touch with the real world; who concerned himself with others and tried to relate to their problems and concerns, especially children. Children were one of Reverend Thomas's specialities. He loved preaching to them and about them, indeed two books of his sermons for children were published in the 1930s by the Epworth Press. Helena still has copies of them, with personal dedications to her.

One was called *Traffic Light: Thirty-Three Parable Stories for Children*, and included three temperance addresses by Reverend Thomas. The book's title comes from its first story, which is typical of many of them in style and purpose. Most start with a human-interest incident the Reverend has read about in the newspapers, in this case *The Times*, which he uses to catch his audience's attention, before moving on to the uplifting moral message. It's a trick clergymen have been using for centuries and one that is still very popular on Radio 4's *Thought for the Day*.

This first story concerns a horse that has run wild in the middle of London. It is tearing along the streets at a furious pace. People shout and wave their arms, motorists hoot their horns, but the horse keeps running, until suddenly, miraculously, it comes to some traffic lights just as they are turning red, and lo and behold, it stops dead. What fun Alan Bennett would have had in his *Beyond the Fringe* days, solemnly telling this little story, then moving on to its moral: 'Now you may well agree that this is a remarkable horse,' Reverend Thomas writes, 'You may wonder if it is true. I don't know about that. I only repeat it as I read it.' This doesn't stop him going on to say that we all have red lights in our lives, such as the Ten Commandments, and that we all have a red light 'which shines in our hearts at certain times, when it is time to go to church or say our prayers'.

Reverend Thomas was clearly a lively, concerned cleric who was a good, caring father. He was teetotal, hence his recurring temperance messages, but he made sure his two adopted daughters had lots of fun in their lives, or what was considered fun in a good Christian family of the 1930s: brisk walks together, active family summer holidays in Devon and a Christmas trip to Oxford Street to admire the lights and enjoy Selfridges' window displays. On Sundays, they were not allowed to play games, ride their bikes, or even knit and sew, but then well-brought-up children in the 1930s had to treat Sundays as a holy day of rest, whether or not their father was a cleric. They did of course go to church each Sunday to listen to their father's services. They remember the church as always packed with a large, very active, mainly middle-class congregation.

In the early years, when they were still quite young, they left halfway through their father's adult services, before he got to his sermon, which did tend to be rather long. A parishoner would bring them home and deliver them to the care of the maid, who would be busy preparing the family's big Sunday dinner.

Reverend Thomas and his wife always had a maid, as did most of the middle classes of the time. She lived in the upstairs attic bedroom of their manse and cooked and cleaned for the family. The only bad experience that Helena can remember from her childhood concerns one maid in particular — Mabel: 'Mabel was there when I arrived — when I was adopted — at least she was the first maid I can clearly remember. Each Sunday the same thing happened. We would be brought back home during my father's service by a member of the church and handed over to Mabel in the kitchen. Then she would tie my hands and legs, pull down my knickers and spank me. There was never any reason. She just didn't like me. She never hit Pam, just me. Poor Pam just had to stand there and watch her beating me.

'I was too scared to tell my mother. I thought Mabel would beat me more if I told on her. This happened every Sunday from when I was about two years old until I was seven or eight, which was when Mabel left. After she'd gone, I did tell my mother, who was horrified I hadn't done so earlier. Today, we would call it child abuse. I presume she was some sort of sadist.'

Apart from this unpleasant weekly incident, which one would hope modern social workers would have detected, Helena was blithely happy in the Thomas household.

Helena and Pam were sent to a small,

fee-paying preparatory school called Norfolk House in north London and, at eleven years of age, Pam went on to the Queen Elizabeth Grammar School for Girls in Barnet, which was considered one of the best schools for girls in north London. Helena joined her there when she was only eight, because by then the war had started and it was decided that the sisters should be kept together.

'I remember the war breaking out, listening to it on the wireless,' says Helena. 'My father had one in the sitting room beside the fireplace. When I was little I used to go behind it to see where the voice was coming from.

'Next door to us lived a family who were Plymouth Brethren. They were very strict and never listened to their wireless on Sunday. Neither did we, apart from the news. We all knew war was imminent, but they still didn't listen. I remember them coming to our house to ask us to come and tell them when we heard war had been declared, because they would not be listening. My mother thought that was a bit of a cheek.'

During the war their father joined the ARP and during bombing raids cycled around Barnet with a tin hat on and a whistle in his mouth, warning people to take cover.

'I used to sit under the stairs, shaking like a jelly,' Helena recalls. 'We had bombs falling in the street, but we never got a direct hit. The worst was when our front door blew off and the roof rose a few inches, then came down again.'

Despite the war, their middle-class, suburban life went on very much in the same way, with tennis parties, picnics and walks in the park until late at night: 'In the war, we had double summer time, which was lovely. It meant you could play tennis until ten at night. At school, we would take a pillow and for an hour in the middle of the day we would have a rest. The theory was we'd probably had a disturbed night with the bombing. I don't remember rationing as being too annoying. It was just a fact of life. I can still see my father with a Mars Bar, which he'd somehow managed to get hold of, cutting it up into tiny slices and giving us one little piece each a day.'

★   ★   ★

From the very beginning, Helena and Pam had been brought up knowing they were adopted. It was no secret to either of them. Everyone in their father's congregation knew as well. This was unusual at the time, but then their father was a minister who didn't lie or pretend, who wanted to be honest and open, and who also probably knew from his study of children and his education, reading and intuition, that this was the best approach to take.

Helena, however, was never told very much about her Hodder family's background — her parents probably knew very little about it. They did tell her she was a triplet and that her mother had died, but she never knew her real name, or where her parents had lived, or what her birth father did for a living.

'What they mainly told me was that I was special. I had been specially chosen. So I just accepted it. I didn't wonder or worry about it, either way. At school I told my special friends, but that was about all. Not because I was keeping it a secret. There was just no need to tell everyone I was adopted. But there was no shame, none at all.

'I never discussed it with my father or mother. I was special, and that was it. Perhaps at the back of my mind I sensed it was a delicate subject. I would never, for example, have said to my mother, 'Why didn't you have children of your own?' I assumed, I suppose, as I got older, that it was my mother's fault, which is, of course, unfair.

'The only thing I did wonder about was whether I was really a triplet. I realised that would be most unusual — you never came across triplets in those days. I also became aware, as I grew up, that when triplets were born they rarely survived. So I did wonder if it was true. If so, were the others alive? But that was only an occasional thought. It didn't really bother me, either way.'

When Helena was sixteen she was not considered quite academic enough to go on to further studies, despite her first-rate school and such a well-educated father. All she could think of doing was something connected with children. 'From when I was very young I'd always said I wanted to work with children, but I didn't know as what. I don't think it was to do with being

70

adopted. It was just how I felt.'

So, in 1949, Helena left her north London private school and prepared to go out into the world.

6

John's Adoption

John William Hodder, the third of the triplets, was the last to be adopted. Being a boy may have been a factor: the thinking is that girls are easier to bring up, that girls will stay closer to their families, that girls are more likely to look after their parents. But the delay may also have been connected to his poor health: at the time the four older Hodders went off to Barnardo's, John was suffering from enteritis and was the one who seemed least likely to survive.

John was three and a half years old when Walter Welburn and his wife Ivy came down to London from Yorkshire to visit the National Adoption Society. By then the society had had him 'on offer' for at least eighteen months, perhaps longer unofficially, if the story about Wills appealing through the pages of the *Daily Mirror* is correct.

John was formally adopted on 30 September 1935, at the county court in the borough of Beverley in Yorkshire. Because of his age he must have been aware, and rather confused, that he was no longer being called John or William, his two birth names, but was now David (his full name became David John William Welburn). Today he can't recall the name change happening or how he felt about it at the time:

CERTIFIED COPY of an Entry in the ADOPTED CHILDREN REGISTER

(16 & 17 Geo. V.; cap. 29).

Given at the GENERAL REGISTER OFFICE, SOMERSET HOUSE, LONDON.

Application Number A.C.R.22118

No. of Entry	Date of Birth	Name of Adopted Child	Sex of Adopted Child	Name, Surname, Address and Occupation of Adopter or Adopters	Date of Birth of Child (if previously ascertained)	Date of Adoption Order and Description of Court by which made	Date of Entry and Signature of Officer deputed by Registrar General to attest the Entry
46691	Seventh October 1935	David John William	Male	Walter Welburn 5 Admiral Walker Road Beverley East Riding of the County of York (a Grocer) Ivy Doris Welburn wife of above of the same address	Eighteenth May 1932	Thirtieth September 1935 The Court in the Borough of Beverley East Riding of the County of York	John R. Watts 1935

CERTIFIED to be a true Copy of an Entry in the Adopted Children Register Maintained at the General Register Office.

Given at the GENERAL REGISTER OFFICE, SOMERSET HOUSE, LONDON, under the Seal of the said Office, the 16th day of October 1935.

This Certificate is issued in pursuance of and subject to the following Acts—16 & 17 Geo. V. cap. 29, sec. 17 & 21; 13 & 14 Geo. V. cap. 27, secs. 1, 2 & 4 and the Adoption of Children (Regulation) Act, 1939, sec. 12. Sub-section (3) of Section 21 of the former Act provides that any certified copy of an entry in the Adopted Children Register, if purporting to be sealed or stamped with the seal of the General Register Office shall be received as evidence of the adoption to which it relates without any further or other proof of such Entry; and no certified copy purporting to be given in the Adopted Children Register shall be of any evidence of the birth of the adopted child unless the entry in the Adopted Children Register contains a record of the date of birth of the adopted child, and where the entry contains a record of the date of birth of the adopted child, such Certified Copy shall also be received as evidence of the date of birth of the adopted child in all respects as though the same were a Certified Copy of an Entry in the Register of Births.

Caution.—Any person who (1) falsifies any of the particulars on this Certificate, or (2) uses a falsified Certificate as true, knowing it to be false, is liable to Prosecution.

A 1248

'The first memory I have is of being taken to see my grandmother in Beverley. I went with my parents and their dog. When we got to my grandma's house, she opened the door and said the dog could come in, but I couldn't.'

David laughs at this story, which was often repeated to him by his family as he grew up. Despite this inauspicious first meeting, he always got on well with his grandmother. He assumes now that she had not been told that his mother was going to adopt a baby, or had been told and been against it.

Walter Welburn was born on 30 April 1896, his wife Ivy Doris Jemima Lightowler on 31 January 1901. They met while they were both working in a baker's shop in Beverley. Ivy was serving on the counter; Walter was working in the back as a baker. In his early thirties he set up on his own as a grocer, along with a partner called Stanley Glenton. From his photographs he appears small, bespectacled, unassuming. People who remember him and his shop, which closed in 1964, say he was quiet and hard-working. As the business prospered he became quite well known in the town, later becoming a town councillor.

Walter and Ivy got married on 25 August 1928. No children came along, so in 1935 they decided to adopt. Perhaps Walter himself was quite happy to secure a boy, hoping he might eventually take over the business. They never did have any children of their own, nor did they adopt any more, so, unlike Gill and Helena, David was brought up as an only child.

He has a colour photograph of himself just after the Welburns adopted him. His fair hair is well brushed, his cheeks chubby — there are no signs of ill health or malnutrition — and he's wearing a striped, woolly, buttoned-up jumper. It appears to be a professional studio photograph, but the label on the back has been torn. All that can be read is '2/6' and 'Head office — Oxford Street, London'. This might well have been an official snap done by the Adoption Society.

He has another picture taken when he was a little older, perhaps the following spring or summer, on the beach at Bridlington. In this one he is standing on the sand with his spade, his hair dishevelled, giving a toothy grin. His face now appears thinner, his eyes a bit sunken, his ears sticking out more, but he is certainly very smiley and happy-looking, which he says he was. Like Gill and Helena, he has only happy memories of his childhood and growing up with his adopted parents.

Walter and Ivy were living in Admiral Walker Road when David was adopted and this is their address on his adoption certificate. They later bought a bungalow in the Leazes, but didn't stay there long as it turned out to have rats. They then moved to a flat above Browns, a clothes shop in Market Place. It's surprising they didn't move somewhere grander since, at its height, Welburn and Glenton grocers was employing six assistants. Perhaps the profits were never as handsome as some people assumed.

David's second memory dates from about the age of four when he caused his mother Ivy to panic when he somehow managed to shove a stone up his nose. It got lodged and stuck. His mother rushed to a neighbour for help and together they laid him on the floor and poured olive oil up his nose, until eventually the stone fell out.

When he was four David went to Minster Infants' School and then aged eight he went into Minster Boys, an ordinary state secondary school. Each summer, his parents took him to Scarborough for a fortnight's holiday where they played on the beach, went putting, rowed on a lake and sometimes visited the theatre in the evening.

★   ★   ★

David was brought up to believe that he was Walter and Ivy's real child, that they were his real mother and father, and David had always been his real name. But an incident occurred when he was about six or seven which always stuck in his mind.

'I was often in scrapes at school, fighting with other boys, and on this particular day one boy I'd had a fight with turned and said to me that I was divorced. When I came home, I told my mam what had happened — that this boy had said I was divorced. I asked her what that meant. Mam just laughed it off. She told me he was being silly, to forget it. I suppose she twigged what had happened, that some people locally must have known about me, but she didn't want to tell me the truth. So, she never did. But all the same it did lodge at the back of my brain.'

Like his sisters, David has vivid memories of being a child during the war: 'I used to look out of my bedroom window and watch Hull on fire. I could see the German planes about eight miles away dropping their bombs, then the sky over Hull would go all red.'

At home, they had a metal air-raid shelter which was kept over the dining table. Some nights all three of them crept under it. When not in use, he played table tennis on it.

Like Gill and Helena, he was pretty average academically. He has no memory of sitting any exam or trying for the grammar school, assuming he wasn't considered clever enough. He loved sport — football and cricket especially — and was captain of the school teams. He was also in the Minster choir for a while, but never liked it. He did enjoy the Church Lads' Brigade, of which he was a member. He remembers his mother doing a lot of knitting and going to meetings of the Young Wives' Guild. His father was mostly busy in the shop, working long hours. He loved them both, he says. They gave him an easy life and spoiled him rotten.

The Welburns had become relatively well off and bought him most things he wanted. He was allowed the sorts of freedom that most children of the time had — to play in the streets and roam the area without too many worries: 'I did go off with a gang of kids once when I was about eight. It was this girl Betty, aged about eleven, who suggested it. She told us to get any money we could from our mams. I got a shilling, without telling my mam what it was for. We all went off for the day to Bridlington on the train, played on the beach all day on our own and didn't get home until six o'clock. By this time Mam was really worried. She got quite angry with me when she saw me safe and sound.'

When David was fourteen, his father came up to his school to ask how David was getting on. 'The headmaster told him I'd do better if I took as much interest in my lessons as I did in sport. The upshot was I stayed on until I was fifteen, but I still didn't pass any exams.

'When I was about to leave Dad asked me what I wanted to do. I said I had no idea. So he asked if I'd like to come into the shop with him. I said no thanks.

'During the war, I'd helped him a bit, but my job had been to sort out the ration coupons for him. Each evening he'd get me to arrange the sugar, butter, cheese, lard and coupons in little piles. I never liked doing it, it was really boring. I thought that would be my full-time job if I went into the shop, that's why I said no.'

Instead his father fixed him up with an apprenticeship with a local builder, Harry Pape. 'Harry had a vacancy for an apprentice bricklayer. I didn't fancy that. I thought it would be too cold in winter. I said I'd rather become a joiner. And that's what happened. I spent the next six years as an apprentice joiner.'

In 1953, when David was twenty-one, he was called up for National Service. It was then that he was finally told by his mother that he was adopted. Perhaps she feared that the army would need lots of official papers. His adoption certificate had been kept by her, and was more than sufficient for normal needs.

'I was having a bath after work, the day the papers came. Mam knew they had come and came into the bathroom. She said she had something important to tell me. I was a bit embarrassed about her coming into the bathroom. I said, 'Can't it wait, Mam, until later?' She said, 'No, I want to tell you something now.' She then told me I was adopted. I told her, 'I know Mam.'

'I didn't really know, of course. It was just that something had lodged in my mind all those years.

'She then told me what she knew, such as it was. She said that she and Dad had gone down to London looking to adopt a baby girl, but when they got there, the girl they had been promised was no longer available. Perhaps she had been withdrawn by her birth mother, as sometimes happened. Anyway, they couldn't go back empty-handed, so they accepted me. I was their second choice, so to speak.

'I don't remember where it was she said she adopted me from. It might have been Dr Barnardo's. I can't remember. That was about all she told me. She said nothing about my parents, my mother dying, me being a triplet. She probably didn't know any of that.

'I didn't ask any questions. I wasn't really bothered. I'd always looked upon them as my mum and dad. It made no difference to me, not really, knowing I was adopted. I've always been easy-going, you might say.'

Not very reassuring, though, to be told you were second choice for your parents. Both Gill and Helena were led to believe they were 'special', which is comforting and pleasing and is still the agreed wisdom as to the approach adopting parents should take. And it is true, in a sense. An adopted child is special, having been picked out, chosen. With a birth child you take what you get, there's no chance of an inspection, no tasting the fruit first.

7

Adoption, the Story So Far

David and Helena were adopted through official legal channels and they have adoption certificates to prove it. Gill's case was less clear-cut, but it must be assumed that the paperwork was done, or problems and confusion would have arisen later on.

If, however, they had been adopted just a few years earlier, none of them would have had any legal documents. Strange as it may seem for such an ancient institution, the first Adoption Act in England and Wales was not passed until 1926, just six years before the Hodder triplets were born.

As we have seen, informal adoption had been carried out by agencies and charities for centuries until 1926. Various acts relating to children's rights and welfare were passed as the years went by, which gave some protection if abuses happened when children ended up in care. (Not every possibility could be covered, as Dr Barnardo found out when he started exporting children to the colonies without the signed approval of their birth mothers.)

Many adoptions were also carried out within families, or between close friends, with no agencies involved. Often adoptions were instigated and carried through by local doctors. The adopting parents could change their new child's name to their own by deed poll and make themselves official guardians without having to worry about any formal adoption law. All that changed after 1926.

The main reason for the 1926 Adoption Act was an increase in illegitimate births during and after the First World War. There were suddenly more babies available for adoption, which in the early 1920s led to a public debate about adoption and the rights and wrongs of introducing a law to govern it. Newspapers ran scare stories about cruel adoptive parents taking advantage of any change in the law that would give them legal powers which they might use for their own ends. On the other side of the coin, it was suggested that 'bad blood' would always out, so adoptive parents were taking a big chance when they legally adopted. The dominant scientific view of the time was that nature would always be stronger than nurture in determining a person's personality.

Meanwhile, lawyers were worried about the Act and its effects on the existing body of family law. There was also the matter of inheritance. If adoption was now to become legally binding, did adopted children have the same rights as birth children to inherit family property, including titles?

Social workers, whose profession was just emerging, were in favour of adoption. Some enthusiastically claimed that it could provide 'the perfect baby for the perfect couple'. It encouraged some psychologists to create tests to prove that babies up for adoption were not only physically appealing, but had the mental talents desired by their prospective parents. This of course can't be done, as they quickly found out.

Finally, after some years of general discussion, theories thrown around, experts offering their experiences, in 1925 the government set up the Tomlin Committee to report on the implications of a new law. It came back in favour of legalising and formalising adoptions, despite misgivings that a change in the law might send the wrong signals to poor families with unwanted children, or encourage unmarried women to have illegitimate babies.

When the 1926 Act was passed, it legally authorised the transferral of a child from one family to another via the courts. In essence the Act simply formalised much that was already being done by various adoption agencies. The courts did not insist on any regulation on the placement, on what might happen afterwards. Their main concern was that the birth parents had legally agreed to the transfer.

The adoption certificate that was issued by the court reproduced almost exactly a birth certificate in design and content. Thus adoptive parents acquired all the rights and duties of birth parents. By the same token, adopted children acquired the same rights as birth children — including inheritance of money and property. (A line was drawn at titles: a baronetcy or peerage could only be passed on to blood relatives.)

Most of the concerns before the Act did not

materialise. There was no evidence of more poor people giving away their babies, or more single women getting pregnant — but then again, little proper research was being done on adoption or its effects.

However, instead, in the years following the passing of the Adoption Act, the whole subject slowly became increasingly unmentionable — a socially unacceptable topic for conversation. Gill and David were typical of most adoptees in the 1930s, in that they were not told the truth about their past until it was forced out of their parents. Helena's were unusual — adoptive parents were encouraged to pass their child off as their own genetic son or daughter. Mostly, there was no guidance at all. It was just accepted that you kept the truth quiet for the good of everyone concerned. Adopted parents just muddled on, most deflecting the subject if it came up — as in David's case — and pretending that it had never happened.

The secrecy which grew up to surround the issue of adoption was based on two social stigmas, two areas of perceived social shame. First, adoptive parents were rarely willing to admit publicly to their infertility. This was probably lurking in the mind of David's grandmother when he first appeared. She didn't want to see this public admission of her daughter's and son-in-law's failure to reproduce.

Second, falling pregnant out of wedlock was, of course, intensely shameful. A girl who was discovered to have done so became a social pariah, a disgrace to herself and her family.

Abortions were dangerous, expensive and hard to secure and the only alternative was to seek sanctuary in 'clinics' of varying respectability, which were either run by charities, or were private, fee-paying places, in order to have the baby delivered in secret. And if the girl went on to marry and have children in wedlock, often she would not want her earlier child to be known about. Adopting parents wanted to keep quiet as much as the birth mother did, to protect the child. So the birth mother, having had the baby in secret, would pass the baby on, also in secret, to strangers she had never met and would never meet, hoping it would remain hidden, for ever.

With such a sense of rather furtive shame attached to adoption, it wasn't surprising that parents worried about upsetting or harming their adopted child by passing on the truth about their beginnings, which would risk making them feel like a second-class citizen.

It's easy to criticise those who tried hard to keep the secret, like David's and Gill's parents, but these social attitudes made it very difficult to be candid. The 1926 Act gave a couple legal guardianship of their new child, with all the rights and duties of real parents. In striving to bring up the child as their own, as the law required, how at the same time could they tell the child the truth? Wouldn't that lead to questions, problems, insecurities? There was also a primitive fear that having revealed the truth, their child might cease to love them and go in search of his or her birth parents.

But of course there was usually some

neighbour or friend who knew the truth. A girl might disappear for a few months before her pregnancy was obvious, concoct a story about where she had been and then return and carry on as normal in her own community, but a woman over the age of thirty who had been married for around ten years with no children would be likely to raise a few eyebrows when she suddenly appeared in the street pushing a pram. David's mother was thirty-four when she adopted David. Emily, Gill's mother, was approaching forty. Obviously, this led to tut-tutting, curtain-twitching, gossip, which other children could pick up on, unaware of its meaning but knowing there was something furtive going on that might provide good ammunition in the playground one day. Gill's experience of being told by some 'friend' in this way was typical of the times.

The Second World War once again greatly increased the number of illegitimate births. During the Blitz, as all contemporary diaries and accounts reveal, people led hedonistic lives — not knowing if they would be alive tomorrow. Normal social and sexual conventions and taboos were ignored. In 1939, there were 31,000 illegitimate births in England and Wales. By 1945 the annual figure had more than doubled to 71,000.

After the war the number of adoptions increased, but not simply because the rise in illegitimate births made more babies available for adoption. There were several other factors. Since the 1926 Act, there had been a marked increase in adoptions by birth parents of their own children born out of wedlock, using the new law to give them legal acceptability and decrease the social stigma of illegitimacy. You were technically no longer illegitimate if you were legally adopted.

Divorce was also becoming easier and less shameful, and remarriage more acceptable. When second marriages occurred, step-parents often used the adoption laws to officially take on the legal responsibility for their partner's previous children.

The peak in the number of adoptions came in 1968 when there were 28,000. But this figure can give the wrong impression, implying that there were 28,000 adoptions along the lines of the Hodder triplets — babies or toddlers adopted by total strangers. In fact around half of those 28,000 were parental adoptions in some form — one of the couple being the birth father or mother of the child being adopted. Adoption figures, like most statistics, have to be understood to be appreciated. While on paper the national trend pointed to more adoptions, the reality was a wider, broader use of the adoption law for reasons which had not quite been envisaged back in 1926.

The next major piece of legislation which had a bearing on adoption and was to have a great effect on the Hodder triplets personally was the 1975 Children Act. This came out of the Houghton Committee report of 1972 which, amongst other things, recommended a clause be inserted to give adoptees over the age of eighteen in England and Wales the entitlement to a copy of their birth certificate. (Since 1930 there had been a provision for this in Scotland.)

During the 1970s, there had been much argument about the advantages and disadvantages of adopted children knowing the truth about their background, about when they should be told, or allowed to find out. The notion of family secrecy, so prevalent in the 30s, 40s and 50s, was now being questioned, as society grew more open and tolerant.

On one side were those who argued that it was a basic human right for a child to know the truth about his or her origins, even at a young age. On the other hand, the truth exposed immature, unformed minds to things they might be unable to comprehend, such as abandonment, perhaps even murder or incest. Surely it was better to protect adopted children from such revelations until they were grown up.

When the Bill was discussed in the House of Commons, there was strong support from a number of MPs for those over eighteen years of age to have access to their original birth certificates. Leo Abse, a Labour backbencher and MP for Pontypool, said: 'Children want an answer to the query, who am I?' Philip Whitehead, another Labour MP and co-sponsor of the Act, argued that more information was important for the adoptee to feel 'psychologically whole'. Mr Whitehead, an adoptee himself, had met his birth mother when he was thirty and said, 'I know that it is a traumatic experience for both parties.'

But there was opposition from some MPs,

notably Conservative MP for Birmingham Edgbaston, Jill Knight, who spoke about the possibility of adoptees 'wrecking another person's life'. This fear was picked up by the popular newspapers, who suggested that vindictive adopted children, having discovered details of their real mother on their birth certificate, would track her down and confront her. MUMS IN FEAR OF KNOCK ON THE DOOR said a headline in the *News of the World*. HAUNTED BY THE PAST blasted the *Daily Mirror*. FEARS OF EMOTIONAL UPSETS OVER 'REVEAL ALL' ADOPTION LAWS warned the *Daily Telegraph*.

The worry was a real one. Someone trying to track down their birth family can find the original or last known location of their mother or father as given on their birth certificate, then ring anyone in the local telephone directory with the same surname. The phone might well be answered by a husband, wife, son or daughter, who is likely to have no knowledge whatsoever about this person from the past.

The 1975 Act did make it possible for those over eighteen to have their birth certificate, but before it was handed over there was a requirement to attend 'counselling interviews' at the social service department of the local authority or the official adoption agency.

The whole subject of adoption had by now become very popular with television and radio, newspapers and women's magazines. Many case histories and human-interest stories were reported and discussed. Letters pages were filled with correspondence on the subject.

By the time the Hodder triplets were adults they had each found out that they were adopted. Gill and Helena were aware, too, that they were one of triplets; David knew nothing of his sisters' existence.

It seemed likely that one of them might be prompted by the prevalence of adoption stories in the media to try to use the new law to begin to establish the truth about themselves. Or would all three continue to be uninterested, unbothered by their pasts?

8

Gill Raises a Family

After the war Gill continued to work with her mother and new father at Rock House, along with Ray and Pearl, her older brother and sister. In the winter, when the guest house was closed, they'd have saved enough money to go off on their own family holiday. Nothing exotic or far-flung, this being the 50s. They usually went to a small hotel in Bournemouth.

Gill's main interest, outside work, was dancing. She went to dance lessons twice a week to learn tap, ballet and musical entertainment. In 1952 she began her own dancing school in Lynmouth — the Gill Rodd School of Dancing, with around sixty young girls and one little boy, Ray's son. She entered her pupils for tap-dancing exams run by the American Tap Dancing Association. Each year the results were printed in the local paper, the *North Devon Journal*. 'Some of my pupils even got gold medals,' recalls Gill.

In the summer of the same year, when Gill was twenty, there was great excitement in the family when her father bought a television — the first one in Lynmouth.

'We had all sat down to watch it for the evening when my boyfriend arrived. He said the river was rising, that there could be floods and he wanted to take me away. I said I wasn't going. I wanted to stay and watch the television.

'At about 9 p.m., Ray came into the front room where we were watching the TV and said the water had reached us. It was coming in through the front door. It was most dramatic. We all left by climbing through the front window and went off to shelter in another guest house, where we spent the night.

'During the night, we could hear the awful noise of the waves and then some terrible crashes. The worse was when the Rhenish Tower collapsed. This was the old beacon on the harbour.'

In the morning, they woke up to find that Rock House was ruined: the whole ground floor had been destroyed. The Rodd family were homeless.

The floods in Lynmouth in August 1952 turned into a national disaster. The whole country watched on TV, if they had one, as rescue operations were mounted. Newspapers devoted many pages to the devastation and the rescue work, with heart-breaking tales of loss and bereavement. Field Marshal Lord Slim came down and directed the rescue work. The Duke of Edinburgh made a visit and so did Harold Macmillan, Minister of Housing. Hundreds of homes and guests homes were ruined. In all, thirty-one people lost their lives in what were some of the worst floods in modern history.

Gill and her family remained homeless for over two years, being forced to stay with relations, then in temporary accommodation, and finally in a council house in Bristol. The family did eventually receive compensation, and bought another guest house in Lynton — Brymoor — which they all moved into and ran from then on.

It was the floods that resulted in Gill losing all her adoption papers. It was not considered a serious loss at the time, certainly nothing compared with the chaos the area was in, but as the years went on Gill began to realise the implications of the loss. She was now totally cut off from her past. She particularly regretted losing the photograph of all three triplets, which Ray said had been in the house and had therefore been destroyed.

★   ★   ★

In 1954 a Scots corporal in the RAF called George Temple arrived in Lynmouth. Originally from Inverness, Jock, as he was known, had joined the RAF as a regular and had been posted to Bridgwater camp in Somerset. On the day he arrived there was some sort of mix-up and they didn't have a bed for him. The sergeant told him that if he wanted to, he could go over to Lynmouth and fill sandbags for a few days. The RAF was helping with flood protection.

Jock didn't actually meet Gill on that occasion, but a few weeks later he came back to Lynmouth with an RAF friend who had picked up a local girl. She was dancing in a show at the Gill Rodd School of Dancing and he suggested Jock came along with him to watch. There he met Gill. Within seven months of meeting they were married, on 7 December 1954 in Lynton. The bold Jock was in his kilt.

Not long afterwards the RAF sent Jock off to Aden. It wasn't until 1956 that he was able to leave the RAF for good and settle down to a less peripatetic life with Gill. He worked as a plumber for a while, then joined the Post Office. In 1957 their daughter Mandy was born.

Like Gill, Jock's family background was rather unusual. His mother had died when he was two so he'd been brought up by his grandmother. His father had then died when Jock was fourteen and this time he was sent to live with another family, with whom he stayed until he was eighteen, old enough to join the RAF. He always felt grateful to the people who had brought him up. Otherwise, so he says, he would probably have been put into a Dr Barnardo's home.

Together, Gill and Jock made the decision not to have another child of their own. Instead, they would adopt and give a loving home and family to someone in need. They felt they wanted to put something back into a society that had helped them in this way, a worthy, altruistic choice which few couples would have made. They knew they could have had more children, so there was then the problem of making sure they didn't, which was not at all easy in the 50s before the advent of the pill. 'Oh, it cost me a fortune in contraceptives,' laughs Jock.

They decided to look for a baby boy as a brother for Mandy and eventually made contact through a church adoption society (which no longer exists) with an eleven-month-old baby boy, Jamie. His mother had been married with two girls, but had had an affair with an Italian waiter which had resulted in a baby and the end of her marriage.

It was all arranged by the adoption society and when Jamie first arrived everything went smoothly at first. But a few months later complications set in.

'The mother was still legally married to the husband and he was furious by what had happened and refused to sign any papers,' says Gill. 'The Italian waiter had returned to Italy and couldn't be contacted. For two years it was awful, with visits from social workers and other people. We began to worry Jamie would be taken away. In the end we contacted our local MP, Jeremy Thorpe. Oh, he was marvellous — I won't have a word said against him. Within forty-eight hours he had got it all sorted out.'

Gill was determined to tell Jamie from the outset that he was adopted. She wanted her son to be told about his origins by his parents, rather than someone in his school playground: 'I told him when he was two and of course he didn't understand. I told him again at five when he went to school. I thought he had taken it in. But when he was about eleven he came home one day and raised the story of Cain and Abel, because some cousins had told him he was adopted. He maintained I hadn't told him and took it very badly. For some time, when I had to tell him off for something or he was in bad mood, he would say, 'You can't tell me what to do. I don't belong to you.'

'But that passed. He's always been a loving son. We are still very close. Only the other day he was telling me that he hopes I'll never die.'

When he was eighteen Jamie decided to find out about his real mother, as the 1976 law had given him the right to do. Gill was uneasy about it and worried how it might turn out. But she didn't want to stop him. His search turned out to be more complicated than he expected. His mother had moved away and got remarried, and it took four years to make contact with her. Then one evening there was a knock at their door. A social worker had arrived to say she had tracked down Jamie's mother. She offered to go and talk to her, to find out if she wanted to hear from Jamie again.

'The message came back that she did, so Jamie went to see her. He found he had three sisters he didn't know about. It was all a shock to him and a bit of a strain. It wasn't at all what he expected. I don't think he would do it again. It was probably a mistake.'

During all this time Gill herself never for one moment felt the same. She still had absolutely no desire to contact her 'real' family, or to know about any possible relations. She knew she was a triplet and that she had had at least four older brothers and sisters to whom Christmas presents had been sent.

'But I didn't want to know any more. I'd had

such a happy upbringing. I loved all my family, all the time. I just wanted things left as they were. I suppose I was worried I might find out about things which might be upsetting. I didn't want anything to change in my life.'

9

Helena Enters the Real World

When Helena was sixteen her father, Reverend Eric Thomas, found out about a training course that might suit her. He got a leaflet from the Methodist-run National Children's Homes, who were looking for girls of sixteen to train as cadets. These homes were run along similar lines to Dr Barnardo's Girls' Village Homes: each housed a group of twenty or so girls aged from three to sixteen and had a sister in charge. The sisters were assisted by two cadets, aged from sixteen to eighteen years of age. They helped in the house while receiving training and lessons in childcare.

Helena was sent first to the Princess Alice School in Sutton Coldfield, where she worked for £2.50 a month. After two years as a cadet, she then went to a training college for sisters in Highbury, north London, where she studied for a year, sat exams and was ordained — as it was termed — to finally become a fully fledged sister.

Finally she moved to a National Children's Home in Oxfordshire called Penshurst, which specialised in caring for handicapped children. Sister Helena had eight girls in her care, seven of them with physical or mental handicaps. She got paid £6 a month and lived in.

'I was pretty much cut off from the real world,'

NATIONAL CHILDREN'S HOME

STEPHENSON HALL
SISTERS' TRAINING COLLEGE

HIGHBURY PARK, LONDON, N.5

This is to certify

that

Helen Thomas

satisfactorily completed her course of
study and practice at the Sisters'
Training College of the National
Children's Home during the year

26.9.52   to   22.9.53

Signed *John W. Waterhouse.*

Principal

Date 23.9.53

Helena says. 'But then I'd always led a very sheltered life, being brought up in a manse. I was naïve, so innocent. I knew nothing about boys. I didn't know about anything going on in the outside world. I never read the newspapers. I wouldn't recommend that sort of life to anyone.'

From the age of sixteen until her late twenties Helena's only excitement was her one afternoon off a week, when she would go into Oxford or Stratford-on-Avon, look around the shop windows, then buy herself a cake. 'I loved cakes. My favourite was a Kunzel Cake. They were the big treat in my life.'

Until she met Harry Minter. He was a previous inhabitant of the Penshurst home, who came back to help out with the children for the summer fête, on Guy Fawkes' night and for the Christmas party. Harry suffered from haemophilia, which was a most debilitating condition in those days. He would get sudden chest pains caused by internal bleeding and every two weeks had to have a complete blood transfusion, which meant he was constantly in and out of hospital.

His father, who had long since disappeared, had been a street musician. Harry's mother had been unable to cope as a single parent and he had been put into care from a young age. On leaving Penshurst at sixteen he had gone to live with his mother in Hackney and had trained as a printer. Treatment for haemophiliacs gradually improved, and as he grew older he managed to lead a relatively normal life.

Helena first met Harry in 1953 on one of his annual visits. The next year they got a bit friendlier and the romance, such as it was, continued at long distance, until in 1959 they got engaged. They finally got married in 1960.

Both her parents were against the marriage, Helena says: 'They said I didn't know what I was taking on. They were just thinking of me. I don't think they really understood what haemophilia was. I suppose they thought we might not be

100

able to have children, thinking of their own situation. Not that they ever discussed such things with me.'

Helena and Harry were married at the Methodist church in Chipping Norton. The reception was at the home and all her charges came along. They didn't have a honeymoon — Harry had just been very ill and was down to seven stone.

Helena gave in her notice and she and Harry set up house on their own in Hackney, near his mother. They bought a little terrace house in Lavender Grove, which cost them £3500 in 1960. At last, aged twenty-eight, Helena had arrived in the real world and was forced to get to grips with everyday, working-class life. Hackney came as a bit of a shock after her leafy, middle-class life in Barnet as daughter of the manse, and the cloistered seclusion of Penshurst. She even started to read the newspapers.

'I read in a paper one day about a prostitute. I had to ask Harry what it meant. That was how naïve I was.'

They had three children: Maryon was born in 1961, Collette in 1962 and Stanley in 1965. Helena had always said she wanted four children, but after their third she and Harry discussed the idea of adopting. Like Gill and Jock they wanted to pay back some of the love they had been given as adoptees in their own childhoods. But Helena then fell pregnant and miscarried, and after that they abandoned the idea.

In 1970 Harry's firm moved to Sidcup in

Kent. The Minters decided to move as well, and they bought a semi-detached house in Sidcup for £5000. Although Helena didn't know it, she had returned to the county of her birth. She was not far away from Sevenoaks, where her real parents had lived and where her six older brothers and sisters, none of whom she even knew existed, were at the time still living and working. Whenever she went shopping she could easily have passed one of them in the street, without ever being aware of it.

But, like Gill, she had no interest in finding out anything about her family background, even when her sister Pam decided to find out a bit about her own birth family in Scotland.

'Pam told me she was trying, but swore me to secrecy. She didn't want our father to find out, so he was never told. But I wasn't interested. I'd had such a happy childhood, I just had no desire to find out who my real parents had been.'

As her own children grew up, she told them she had been adopted. Collette was particularly fascinated and plagued her mother for more information. But she had none to give.

'I just could never understand it,' says Collette. 'How could she not want to know? All she knew was that she was a triplet. But she didn't even know if the other two triplets had been boys or girls. I mean how could anyone go through life not wanting to find out? It seemed crazy to me, perverse.'

10

David Becomes a Mormon

In 1953 David was called up for National Service. He joined the Royal Engineers, being sent first to Great Malvern for two weeks, to Elgin in Scotland for four months, then to Osnabrück in Germany where he remained for the rest of his military service.

'I loved it,' he says. 'It made me, really. I became independent. I spent most of my time in the army playing sport, mainly boxing. I boxed at nine stone and was the regiment's bantam-weight champion. I never rose higher than a private, I didn't want to. But I loved every minute of it.

'When I came out, I went to see Harry Pape, my old employer. He said he'd take me on again but I said, 'No, I'm not coming back. I'm going out into the world.'

'I didn't actually go very far. I got a job ten miles away at Brough, near Hull, in an aircraft factory.' The factory, which was called the Blackburn Aircraft Company, later became part of British Aerospace.

Eighteen months later David met a girl in the factory:

'She was working on a bench not far away. I said to my mate on the bench beside me, 'I wouldn't mind taking that lass out.' This was on the Monday. On the Friday morning, he says to me, 'Well, then, have you asked her?' I said no. He said if I hadn't asked her by dinner, he'd ask her for me.

'Well, I wasn't having that. So I went across to her bench very sheepishly and asked her if she'd like to come to the pictures with me. I went as red as a beetroot. That was probably why she didn't turn me down.'

The girl's name was Margaret Green and that night David did indeed take her to the cinema. After that they went out a couple more times and David confessed that he had been adopted. Margaret also had a confession to make. She already had a son, Kevin, aged two. He was in a Dr Barnardo's home as she could not bring him up on her own and go out to work. She was living alone in a rented room at the time. 'I said it was fine about her baby. It didn't bother me at all.'

David and Margaret had been going out for about eighteen months when they heard that a two-up, two-down house in Beverley was up for renting. David's wage at the time was more than enough to pay the rent, so they decided to get married. 'It just sort of happened. It just seemed the obvious thing to do.'

They got married on 29 March 1958, and immediately afterwards Kevin, now aged three, left his Barnardo's home and came to live with them permanently. He was then officially adopted by David — an example of legal adoption within families distorting adoption statistics.

David and Margaret did not tell Kevin that he had been adopted, that David was not his real father. A generation later history had repeated itself. David can't remember their reasoning now. He says he thinks they just never got round to it, and anyway Margaret was his real mother after all.

Kevin found out the truth when he was about twelve years old in the usual way: he had an argument at school with a boy, whose weapon was to tell Kevin that David was not his real father. Of course, when their son came home that night he confronted David and Margaret, who had to admit it was true. Kevin says it didn't really worry him. Like David, he was not much bothered.

David and Margaret went on to have two children of their own: Elizabeth, born in 1959, and John, born in 1962. By now they were living in an ex-vicarage in Hull, but two years later they moved again — to a bigger house, also in Hull, where Margaret became pregnant with their fourth child. Sadly, like Helena, she miscarried. She couldn't bear living in the house after that, so they sold it and moved into a rented maisonette nearby.

One day in 1964 David came home from work to find that his wife had had visitors. Two young, smartly dressed American gentlemen had come to the front door and asked Margaret if she was interested in finding out about their church. She had asked them to come back when her husband was at home.

'When they arrived,' says David, 'they were

both wearing smart suits and trilbies and looked to me like gangsters. They talked about their church, Jesus Christ of the Latter-Day Saints — the Mormons. Margaret was interested, but I wasn't.'

Indeed Margaret decided to join the Mormons, who had recently opened a church in Beverley, and over the next six months they were often about the house.

'One day, when they were here,' David remembers, 'I happened to be wallpapering the bedroom. One of them came up and said he'd help me. After we'd finished, he said, 'I've helped you with the wallpapering, so will you give me ten minutes and I'll tell you about our church?' I'd been conned, really — that was what he'd wanted to do all along. So I gave him ten minutes, and the upshot was I got converted. I became a Mormon, and that was how we brought up our three children.'

Mormons are fascinated by genealogy, which stems from the church's preoccupation with saving the souls of dead ancestors. Mormon churches around the world tend to have immaculately-kept local archives and personal family histories. Whether Margaret was already interested in such things before she became a Mormon or afterwards is not clear, but she had always shown a keen interest in keeping records (she had kept careful notes on the exact details of all the family's house moves, for example).

When she married David, she knew, of course, that he was adopted, but that he had never bothered to get a copy of his original birth certificate. So in 1961, while on a trip to London, Margaret decided to take her husband to Somerset House to do some research on his family history.

When they arrived at the office of the Registrar General they managed to get a copy of David's original birth certificate. Margaret noticed immediately that the certificate gave a time as well as a date for her husband's birth. She was told that this was an indication David was one of a multiple birth. 'We enquired whether they had the other birth certificate. Minutes later someone returned and asked us, 'Which one do you want? We've got two.' We were very shocked.'

David, the only one of the triplets who had no idea he had siblings of any kind, let alone ones with whom he had shared a womb, had become the first to set eyes on the original documentation with vital clues to his origins and real family connections.

The two remaining certificates revealed the existence of his sisters Florence and May. May's read, 'Adopted: L. J. Stone, Deputy Superintendent Registrar'. Florence's lacked any such details, of course. Neither did they contain the names of, or information on the families who had adopted his sisters. There was no way the documents could help them to find out what had happened to his sisters — who had adopted them or where they lived.

David's birth certificate also gave the names of his parents, the Hodders, and where they were living at the time of his birth — Forge Cottage,

Seal Chart. This was now over thirty years earlier so they presumed there was little chance that they would still be there, or even alive.

When they returned home Margaret did send a few letters to Seal Chart, but got no replies. It is always hard for amateurs with no training in tracing people and little money, to know how to go about such matters. The couple did not have the funds to travel from Yorkshire to Seal Chart in Kent especially to make investigations, which might not lead anywhere. They had reached a dead end as far as the trail of David's family was concerned.

But Margaret had now been sparked off to trace her own ancestry. Helped by her Mormon friends, she went to local libraries and wrote off for copies of the birth and death certificates of her own family. She managed to trace them back three generations, but continued to draw blanks with David's.

★　★　★

In 1970 Margaret got itchy feet again, despite all their house moves. This time she was interested in pastures much further afield. She had a friend who had emigrated to Australia and on a visit back home she told Margaret about the wonderful life out there. Margaret decided she would like to join her.

'It was Margaret's decision,' says David. 'She was always the boss — we fell into line. The Australian government had a special scheme for tradesmen who wanted to emigrate. You only had to pay £10 for your passage — one way, of course. All you had to do was get fixed up with a job and agree to stay for at least two years.'

Their children were still quite young at the time. Kevin was fourteen, Elizabeth eleven and John eight. They did worry about taking them away from all their schoolfriends, but on the other hand, this was a big adventure for all of them. 'I thought, why not? I'll give it a go,' says David.

So in November 1970 David, Margaret and their three children emigrated to Australia, for good, as far as they knew. If either of his triplet sisters or any of his Hodder relations had wanted to contact him, which so far they had not, it would have been hard enough to track him down in Beverley, Yorkshire. But by going off to Australia, he was almost certainly bringing to an end any remote chance of finding, or being found by any of his blood relations.

11

Interlude on the Hodders

The triplets' lack of knowledge of their origins, their blood relations and their family heritage meant that it was unlikely any one of them would spark off a successful, sustained search for their parents, or any of their siblings. But what of Wills and his other offspring?

In 1934, after his family had been split up, Wills had moved with his younger children, Pat and Jean, to live with his parents in Post Office Cottage in Seal Chart. At this point he knew the whereabouts of just one of the triplets — Gill. But once her adopted mother Emily had rejected his proposal of marriage he gave up going to visit both of them, and had soon lost all contact with even her.

By the time the Second World War came, Wills' four other children, Evelyn, Kath, Ron and Joe, had come out of their Barnardo's homes. Both boys joined the armed forces: Ron went into the army and Joe decided on the navy. They survived the war unscathed, and in 1945 they returned to Seal Chart to live with their father and grandparents at Post Office Cottage with Pat and Jean, who had both become local farm-workers on leaving school.

The two older sisters, Kath and Evelyn, had gone from domestic service into war service, after which they had gone their different ways. Kath got married and moved to Winchester; Evelyn went to live with Aunt Florrie in Harrow, where she got a job on the conveyor belt at the Hoover factory.

'We often talked about what had become of the triplets,' says Florrie. 'Evelyn really became obsessed by them, going on all the time, wondering about them.

'In 1952, of course, we read about the awful floods in Devon and we did wonder if Gill was still alive or not. But we didn't know how to contact her.'

For many years, she says, she and Evelyn did try to find out what had happened to the other triplets. Every time there was a story in the newspapers or on the radio about adopted children being reunited, they would ring or write, saying they were looking for long-lost triplets.

'I contacted Charlie Chester's show on Radio 2 and they said they would mention it, but I don't think they did. Evelyn and I went up to the *Daily Mirror* offices one day to look through their files. We had this memory of a photograph of the triplets being in their paper, but we didn't find nothing.'

Wills died in April 1963, aged sixty-seven. According to Florrie, his last words were to wonder what had happened to his triplets. His death left Ron, Joe, Pat and Jean living in the family house. Ron and Joe worked in the building trade; Pat and Jean carried on as farm-workers and by the mid 1970s all four of

111

them were still living happily together, each unmarried. They all remembered the triplets, but none of them appears to have ever made any attempt to track them down. Only their sister Evelyn, up in Harrow, ever showed a real interest in knowing what happened to them, but for now her efforts to trace them had proved as fruitless as Margaret's.

12

Elspeth's Story

It might seem strange that the Hodder triplets showed little interest in finding out about their birth family. Even when each knew they were one of triplets, the information scarcely kept them awake at night. David was surprised but not unduly bothered; Gill and Helena had always known and had no wish to delve into the past. Their given reasons were a mixture of fear of the unknown and a sense of loyalty to their adopted parents, which are understandable.

Evelyn, on the other hand, had always wanted to solve the family mystery. After all, she had seen their father go to his grave having not seen his triplets past the age of one, never knowing where they had ended up. Evelyn knew that there was nothing to fear in going back to the past: her parents had been poor but good, honest people. She envisaged that a future reunion, when and if it took place, would be joyous.

David's wife Margaret, too, was interested, but more as part of a general interest in social and family histories. She was fascinated by the idea of searching for the truth about David's birth and his forebears, but her concern was not an obsession fed by the aching curiosity you may have if it is your own flesh and blood for which you are searching.

Adopted people often do feel this ache. They lie awake wondering why they are as they are; where their character and features have come from; who their parents were; if they had any brothers and sisters; what they might look like; whether they are alive and well; and where they are now. Without this knowledge they can feel disconnected and lack an inherent sense of belonging anywhere, even if they are perfectly happy with the family who brought them up. They might not want to search for their birth parents, or they might wait many years, until perhaps something happens to change their mind. But the possibility is rarely far from their mind, floating in their dreams, ever present in their waking reveries.

There is a romance about adoption. The idea of it can attract even children who aren't adopted. My wife, Margaret, for example, used to fantasise as a little girl that her father was not her real father — her real father would of course turn out to be Prince Charming. This way she would not be condemned for ever to the council house in which she was brought up. She had always felt she didn't belong to the situation and family in which she found herself, though she did dearly love her mother. It's a common daydream, popular in myths and legends and fairytales.

Perhaps in the case of the triplets, it was not just fear and respect that held them back, but also a lack of the sort of imagination that makes people wonder about themselves, wonder how things could be better, or different. They

114

proclaimed themselves happy with life as it had turned out and this limited them, made them refuse to dwell on the possibilities — good or bad — that knowledge of the past could bring.

★ ★ ★

Elspeth, a distant relation of mine, is just a few years younger than the triplets. She was adopted in 1936 when only a few weeks old by a farm-worker and his wife in Ayrshire and she has spent a lifetime wanting to know the truth about herself.

She has a memory dating back to when she was about six or seven years old. She was at the village school and was having an argument with another child in the cloakroom. He finally shot back to her, 'You're a wee bastard.' Like David and Gill she sensed this was not an empty insult, but didn't quite know what it meant. However, she didn't ask and it was not discussed again, until she was fourteen. It was then her mother told her she was adopted. Few details were known, so her mother said, apart from the fact that she had been found through a church agency in Manchester.

Elspeth grew up to be artistic and musical, quite unlike her adopted parents. She was tall, dark-haired and strikingly pretty, while her parents were ginger and mousy, very fair-skinned and rather squat and lumpy. She felt very little in common with them, but her childhood was happy enough and she was grateful to them for her stable upbringing.

When she left school Elspeth went to a teachers' training college in Glasgow, where she met and then married Tucky from the Highlands. He was an engineer with an international oil company and they spent over twenty years living abroad. She taught in international schools, taking time off to have a boy and a girl. Her husband eventually took early retirement and they returned to Britain. Six years ago she was diagnosed with diabetes, and during various tests for the condition she was asked if there was any history of diabetes in the family. Of course, she didn't know.

Soon after this diagnosis she stayed with us in London. During her stay she told my wife she was adopted. Margaret was fascinated, as she always has been by adoption, and asked why Elspeth had never tried to trace her real parents. She replied that since she'd known she was adopted, she had never stopped thinking about them.

'As a child, I longed each evening before going to sleep for a brother or a sister. I never told my mother this, it just nagged away in my mind. I knew I didn't belong in this family, even before I knew the truth. I felt like a cuckoo in the nest. I loved them dearly, they were so good to me, couldn't have been more loving. They did try so very hard, taking me to music lessons when they had no interest in music, letting me go on school trips to France when they had so little money. I didn't want to meet my real mother and other relations, so I told myself, I just wanted to know about them, see their photographs, know the

116

facts about them. Like painting by numbers. I wanted help to fill in some of the colours and details. That way I would be able to give myself an identity, a proper existence. I didn't have to meet them — just know about them. So I told myself. But of course I fantasised all the time about what they would really look like.

'When I had my children, it was such a thrill to have created my own family, people that were part of me. I had blood relations at last. I know with some adopted people that's when they decide to track down their real parents, but that didn't happen with me. It made me feel more content, not as restless, not as obsessed. Anyway, I didn't want to do anything while my parents were still alive.'

Over the years, Elspeth had picked up from her adopted mother that her real mother had been some sort of servant-girl who had been taken advantage of by the master of the house. This rather comforted Elspeth. Her mother understandably could not have kept the child, whom of course she had dearly loved, while the father was probably very wealthy, perhaps even someone titled or famous.

Her father had since died but her mother was still alive, though very frail. However, whilst Elspeth was with us, her mother did pass away. So Margaret suggested this was perhaps the time for Elspeth to start her search. She was hesitant and half-worried that it still wasn't fair to her adoptive mother, but Margaret said she would make some basic inquiries, see what there was to be found.

Elspeth had a copy of her birth certificate, which showed that her maiden name had been an unusual Scottish one. If her surname had been Smith or Jones, Margaret would not have taken her inquiries any further, but this made it easy. She then had a hunch that Elspeth's mother might have got married in the five years after her birth — perhaps to someone local. She had no reason other than intuition to think this.

'I went to St Catherine's House in the Aldwych to look at the marriage registers,' Margaret says. 'It was full of people making notes, making discoveries. It was all so exciting — I loved going there, just for the atmosphere.

'There are four volumes for every year, arranged alphabetically. They're enormous, of course, as they cover every marriage in England and Wales, but it was easy to skim them because of the unusual surname I was looking for. Within thirty minutes I found that Elspeth's mother had married a man called Anderson just a year after Elspeth was born.

'Having got her married name, I looked up the births for the next two or three years and found she'd subsequently had two boys. I gave all the certificates to Elspeth, so that she could take over, if she wished to.'

For the next five years nothing happened. Elspeth's own children, now grown up, were interested, and one of them tried to do some research on the internet, but found nothing of note.

They also contacted the Mormons, asking them to help. In 2001 they were in touch with

Elspeth to say they had traced her brother. His name was Eric, he lived in Chelsea, London and he was an eminent lawyer. They offered to act as intermediaries if she wanted to take it further and when she agreed they contacted Eric, who was amazed to be told that over sixty years ago his mother had had a child out of wedlock. He knew nothing about it. His mother had always been the soul of conservative respectability as far as he was concerned.

Eric told the Mormons that he didn't want to meet Elspeth at this stage, but she could write to him, which seemed sensible. She did so, giving a bit of her life story and enclosing a photograph. Eric was delighted by her letter, realising she was a bright, intelligent woman and not someone who might cause trouble in his family. He rang her up and suggested they should meet on neutral territory. He chose a restaurant not far from where Elspeth lived in Devon as by chance he had some legal business to do in that area. Eric told nobody about this meeting, not even his own wife, unsure how it would go or where it might lead.

Over the meal, he told Elspeth that he had another full brother — Grant. Their mother was still alive. She was eighty-six and was living at the same address as her marriage certificate gave. She was now a widow — her husband had been much older, and had died many years before. Eric confided to her that he suspected his father was also Elspeth's, which would make her his full sister. Whether or not this was correct, they got on very well. Each was delighted to find a sibling they had never known existed. They felt in tune; physically and emotionally connected.

Eric said he was going to confront his mother with the news of Elspeth's discovery next time he went up to visit her. He said he would contact Elspeth when he had done so, to tell her the outcome.

A few weeks later Elspeth received an outraged letter from Grant, whom she had still not met. Eric had told Grant about Elspeth's sudden appearance, that he was going to confront their mother and Grant had pre-empted Eric by going off at once to see her himself. In the letter he went on to say that when he had asked his mother, point blank, if she had had another child apart from himself and Eric, she had been silent for a while. Finally she had said, 'It was all a long time ago. I don't want to talk about it.' So it was not a denial.

Grant then wrote that he didn't want Elspeth to go anywhere near his mother. It was outrageous for an outsider to suddenly come into the family, stirring up trouble, dragging up the past. If she did contact her, the shock might kill his mother and it would be Elspeth's fault. He also seemed to imply that Elspeth was 'interfering in the family' for some sort of gain, financial or otherwise.

Elspeth was naturally very upset by this. She agonised for several days, wondering whether to tear the letter up and forget the whole thing, or try to contact Grant and explain she had no ulterior motives. She decided in the end to ring him, but he hung up on her.

Eric was aghast at Grant's behaviour. He went to see his mother and also told her about Elspeth. By this time she'd had time to think and was far less upset. She said she would like to meet her daughter.

The big, emotional reunion finally took place in the spring of 2002. At first there was a stiffness, a strangeness between them, as if they had no connection, until eventually Elspeth's mother tearfully explained what had happened back in 1936 when she'd found herself pregnant. Elspeth did not pry too intently as to the full story behind her adoption, allowing her mother to tell only what she wanted to tell. She was very open about her plight back then.

Elspeth's father had been a headmaster and Elspeth's mother his pupil. His marriage was unhappy and they began an affair when she was sixteen. When she became pregnant she had to go into a home for unmarried mothers because her father turned her out. Nobody would help her when Elspeth was born and, absolutely desperate, she had seen the adoption of her daughter as her only choice.

Her lover had managed to get a divorce nearly two years later, and they had got married, going on to have two children. But the existence of their first child, born out of wedlock, was always kept from everyone.

When she had finished the story Elspeth's mother appeared relieved to have finally shared her secret and her guilt. In fact afterwards she began talking about it all the time, telling people who came to visit her about her wonderful daughter who had turned out so well.

Ultimately the reunion had turned out just as Elspeth had dreamt it would. And she had not only gained a mother, but two brothers as well. Having seen his mother's immense pleasure in finding Elspeth, Grant had softened his attitude towards her. Meanwhile Eric and Elspeth have become excellent friends. They are affectionate and demonstrative towards each other, and totally at ease. They do look very similar: they are both tall, dark-haired and attractive, although Elspeth is shy, sensitive and retiring, while Eric is bold and confident.

'I wake up each day smiling at the thought of Eric,' says Elspeth. 'I feel such a whole, completed person. The past didn't turn out to be worrying or nasty, as I'd sometimes feared it would. And the present and future are so lovely. Yes, I do wish it had happened earlier, but I now have so much to look forward to.'

So, a very different situation to that of the triplets. Elspeth had always harboured a desire to know about her family, unlike Gill and Helena. And she was helped by someone who knew how to go about finding them, who pushed her along the path. David's wife Margaret could have played the same role for the triplets, but it seemed unlikely she would do so now, living on the other side of the world.

13

Evelyn Hodder Finds a Brother

David Welburn and his family landed in Melbourne, Australia in November 1970. They lived with friends there for about a month before they decided to buy their own house in sunny Brisbane.

The family were very happy there for the next three years and then in 1973, when Kevin had reached the age of eighteen, he told them he wanted to return to England. They felt they couldn't stop him, now that he was eighteen, so they eventually agreed and he returned to Hull, on his own.

'After a few months,' says David, 'we started getting letters from friends in Hull who said that Kevin was living it up. He was going to pubs and going out with lots of girlfriends. We began to worry about him.'

They were still active Mormons, and had brought up their children as churchgoers, so naturally they were upset by these reports. Kevin smiles today, saying he wasn't up to much. But, of course, having parents who were devout Mormons, anything not strictly on the straight and narrow was likely to alarm them, especially when they were so far away.

In 1974 the family decided they had to come back to England. David is insistent that he was happy with their life in Australia and didn't want to leave, but a family decision was made. 'Margaret was as worried as me,' he says, 'but she wanted us to come back slowly, spending a year over it, going to New Zealand and other places. I said no, we had to go straight back.'

Back in Hull they rented a three-bedroom flat and Kevin moved in with them. 'After about a year,' says David, 'he got married. Oh, we were happy he'd got married, but it meant we hadn't really needed to come home. He wouldn't have come to any harm after all. We could have stayed in Australia. But it was too late. I got my old job back and we decided we'd stay.'

They moved several times, before buying their own house in Beverley. While David returned to British Aerospace, Margaret picked up her interest in genealogy, trying even harder to get to the bottom of David's family history.

'I still wasn't all that interested, myself,' says David. 'But Margaret used to go off to Hull all the time and spend hours in the reference library looking up old records.

'When I had first discovered I was adopted, I had asked Dad about my birth family, but he didn't know much at all. Whenever Margaret brought up the subject, he used to say there was no point trying to track them down. They might be anywhere in the world. They might all have emigrated, or been dead.

'I think the real reason was that he and Mam were worried that if I did find my real family, I might want to go and live near them.'

One day in 1976 Margaret read an article in

Women's Realm magazine about some twins who had been adopted separately at birth and had then been reunited, many years later. She wrote to *Woman's Realm*, telling them about her husband:

I was interested in Maureen Vincent's series on amazing reunions, especially the twins who were reunited. My husband was also adopted, 41 years ago at the age of two years nine months, but with one difference. He was a triplet, the only boy.

He and his sisters were born in Sevenoaks on 18 May 1932, but when their mother died and their father was no longer able to look after them, they had to go to an orphanage. Then they were adopted by different people. My mother-in-law once told me she wanted two of them, but they wouldn't let her have two. They were christened May, Florence and John Hodder. My husband retained both his Christian names and had another name put on the front.

For years we have wanted to get in touch with his sisters, but didn't know where to start. It has always been my husband's ambition to see any nieces or nephews he might have, as he was brought up an only child. We have the original birth certificates of all three. I wonder if any of your readers can help.

Mrs M. W. Hull

A note after the letter added, 'We will forward any replies to Mrs M. W.'

The reference to David's parents' wish to adopt him and another of the triplets is family legend, since of course David was adopted some time after the others.

Three or four months later David came home from work to find that two letters had been sent on from *Woman's Realm*. 'One was from a woman who said she was a friend of the family, but her details were very vague and it was clear she was making them up. But the other letter was from a woman called Evelyn, who claimed she was my sister. She said she wasn't one of the triplets, but an older sister. She said there had been six children born to the family before the triplets.

'Well, this was a shock. It had been a surprise all those years ago finding out I'd been one of triplets. But I never for one moment thought I might also have had another six brothers and sisters.'

David and Margaret replied to Evelyn, who was still working in the Hoover factory in Harrow. They wrote letters, then talked on the phone, and finally arranged to meet.

It turned out that Evelyn had not spotted the *Woman's Realm* letter herself. A cousin had rung her to tell her to buy a copy, knowing Evelyn's obsession with finding the triplets. Evelyn knew immediately that it was genuine. After all these years, one of the triplets had been located.

Evelyn told David that she remembered that

the triplet known as Florence had been adopted by a woman in Devon, but she couldn't remember whether she was called Mrs Davies or Mrs Davey, or whether she lived in Lynmouth or Plymouth. Reaching into the recesses of her memory, she recalled that the dolls she had been sent at Barnardo's at Christmas time had come from a guest house called Rock House.

Evelyn now decided she would send letters both to Rock House, Plymouth and Rock House, Lynmouth to see what happened. In each letter she briefly told the story of the adoption and explained that one triplet had been found and the family wanted to find the other two.

To her surprise, a few weeks later she got a letter back from the vicar of Lynton, Reverend Francis Coles, who advised her that Mrs Davey had died some years ago. However, he said there were other relatives living in the district and if Evelyn could be bothered to write again, giving more details about herself, he would pass the letter on to them.

14

The First Great Reunion

By a great stroke of fortune, not only had Evelyn's letter been read by someone who knew of Mrs Davey, it had actually been received by a member of Gill's family. There had been no Mrs Davey at Rock House since 1946, when Emily Davey had remarried. Emily herself was no longer alive, she had died in 1968, but, by chance, Rock House was still being run by a member of the family: Doreen, the now estranged wife of Raymond, Gill's older brother.

Doreen had opened Evelyn's letter. She remembered that Emily had once been called Mrs Davey and that she had adopted Gill as a baby, so she realised that after all these years someone from Gill's original family had managed to trace Gill. Her first reaction was to destroy the letter to protect Gill from anything unsettling and potentially unpleasant — she didn't want Gill to receive any upsetting news, or begging letters.

For a few days she did nothing. Finally she went over to Brymoor House, where Gill still lived, took aside Jock, Gill's husband, and began to tell him about the letter. A few minutes later Gill happened to come into the kitchen. She heard them whispering and asked what it was all about. They both had to tell her.

'I was shocked,' says Gill. 'Doreen had guessed my feelings. I didn't want to know anything. I didn't want to have any contact. Bygones were bygones — that's how I looked upon it.'

For the next two or three weeks, Gill did nothing. Her eighteen-year-old daughter Mandy was against her mother replying. She resented the fact that she had been approached out of the blue by a total stranger. Neither was Jock keen, fearing there might be some unhappy repercussions.

'I was in a quandary,' says Gill. 'I just couldn't decide what to do. Mandy and Jock were against it, but I wanted to know what Raymond thought, so I rang him. (He had moved away at the time, having separated from Doreen.) He said that part of him was for it, part against. He asked me to give him twenty-four hours to think about it. When he rang back he said, 'Yes, give it a go.'

'My father, the man I always called my father, Richard Rodd, was still alive, although he was very ill at the time and he died just a few weeks later. My sister said that blood is thicker than water, so I should do it, but I still couldn't decide. In the end, I decided to discuss it with Reverend Coles. I knew he had two adopted children of his own, so he would be very sympathetic.

'He offered to write back to Evelyn and try to get some more information before revealing my existence. Depending on her response, we could take it from there.

'Some days later, he rang me and said he'd heard from Evelyn. As far as he could see, she and her family appeared to be perfectly decent and genuine.

'So I took a very deep breath and I replied to Evelyn. Within twenty-four hours I had all the older Hodders ringing me up. It was very overwhelming and confusing. Suddenly I had all these relatives I had never met and knew nothing about. But they all seemed so nice, so I invited them down to the guest house to stay. The first ones to come were Eve and Kath.'

Mandy, Gill's daughter, absented herself during the visit, still worried about it all. Jock also remained concerned, apart from anything else he thought that he might be about to lose Gill in some way.

During the visit from Eve and Kath, they made a day trip to Winchester, where Kath was then living. To Gill's surprise she found that waiting there to meet her were Ron, Joe, Jean and Pat, plus the redoubtable Aunt Florrie, now in her seventies.

But more was to come. She then got a letter from David, her missing triplet, who had been told by Evelyn that Gill had been discovered. So Gill invited him and Margaret to come down and visit them in Lynmouth as well.

'Gill met us off the bus,' says David. 'She gave me a cuddle and right away I knew everything was going to be all right. Any possible tension had been broken.'

They stayed a week and had a great time, meeting Gill's local friends and relations. Then Gill took David and his family to Winchester.

'I didn't know what was coming,' says David.

'It seemed a long way for an outing. When we got to Winchester we walked down the street and I saw a house all decorated with balloons and things. I said, 'Look, someone's having a party.' Gill told me it was the house we were going to. So I walked up the path and Evelyn opened the door. It was the first time I'd ever met her and also my other big sister, Kath. We had a great family party — of course everyone wanted to meet me and Gill.'

★   ★   ★

In theory, having remembered the name Rock House, Evelyn could have tracked down Gill many years before. But until contact was made with David and one triplet had been discovered, she felt she had little to tell Gill, little reason for suggesting they should all meet up again. Margaret had really sparked it all off, by getting her letter into *Woman's Realm*.

In their July 1976 issue *Hoover News* devoted half a page to Evelyn Hodder's triumphant story: 'Two letters — one published by a magazine, the other sent by chance to Devon — have broken a forty-four-year-old silence and ended a lifetime of wondering for Evelyn Hodder, a Perivale assembly line worker.'

The article went on to explain how the triplets had been adopted and had lost contact with each other. It said that Evelyn had now begun a new search for the missing third triplet: 'Evelyn is buoyed with determination to make contact with May now.'

The *Hoover News* scoop finished with a final paragraph: 'When they are all reunited, *Hoover News* will be there. It will be a memorable occasion.'

It was indeed to be a very memorable occasion. But no one could have guessed how long it would take. Another twenty-five years would elapse before all three triplets were finally united.

15

Getting Acquainted

For the next year the Hodder family, with all its extensions, had enough to concern itself with as everyone got to know one another, especially the two triplets for whom it was a time of immense excitement.

'I felt so grateful I had found Gill,' says David. 'And through looking for her, the older brothers and sisters I never knew I had.'

'All my fears turned out groundless,' says Gill. 'I was so pleased to have met up with my family. I loved meeting them all and getting to know them, though for a long time it was very confusing, working out who was who.'

Gill and David established regular contact with the four older Hodder children, still in their grandfather's cottage in Stone Street, and with Kath in Winchester. They often visited one another, went on outings together and wrote to each other quite frequently.

The set-up at Stone Street, with four unmarried brothers and sisters living together, might have been a bit unusual, but Gill says it all worked happily. When they all met up Ron was still working for a builder, Joe was a gardener and Jean and Pat were still farm-workers. 'I could see that Jean had been very attractive,' says Gill. 'I picked up that she'd had lots of boyfriends in the past, but there were none around when I got to know her. She told me that on his deathbed our father had asked her to look after Pat. I'm sure he asked the boys as well, and that's probably why they never married.'

Gill has kept all the letters received from her new relations during that first year. Mostly they are full of day-to-day trivia — how the garden is going, the weather, what the family is doing — but when the reunion itself comes up they are quite emotional as they struggle to express what are clearly very strong reactions. Reading them is especially poignant when you remember that up until now the Hodders had not had much experience of writing down their personal feelings.

In June 1976 Kath wrote to Gill to say that she had by chance visited Lynmouth some years ago.

If only I'd known, we could all have had many happy years together, but I'm so thrilled about it all. If only we could find May. I'm sure she would also be quite like the rest of us. We are all so much alike in nature and looks and it would make your life complete.

I wonder if we find May, if she will approve of us all. It will be a bit of a shock if she doesn't even know any of us exist. She may not even answer any request that Eve makes.

I could hug and kiss you if you were here,

instead I've kissed your letter. I feel so very close to you, Gill, I feel the same way with our Jean, only I can't express my feelings enough. Blood is thicker than water, isn't it? (I shall have to watch — your Jock will be jealous of us!)

It will be nice when you can arrange a few days in Kent and see your natural home, your mother and father's grave, the church where they were married and mother sang in the choir. I love it all, I feel at peace there. Our Anne [her daughter] used to go and sit by Dad's grave when she went to stay with Jean. She used to write poems to Grandad. I've often said that when I die, I want my ashes taken up to that churchyard.

The letters from Joe display a dry sense of humour. In his first one, he begins:

Dear Jill, Jock, Mandy and Jamie,
Having completed the first line, I would like to remind you that letter writing to me is not a profession or an art. It is such an unfamiliar habit, that how writers manage to create books is beyond me.

The writing pad, however, is before me. The pen is in my hand, so I will now endeavour to venture into the unknown.

I can imagine your first reaction, Jill. 'Good heavens, he's actually writing to me, the world is full of surprises.' Give her a brandy, Jock.

In fact, Joe's letters are well written, with good spelling and punctuation. Only the odd word is not quite right and, like all of them, he is not sure whether to spell his sister's name Gill or Jill.

In one letter, he describes his reaction to meeting Gill for the first time at Winchester:

When you stepped out of the car, I knew you. There was no shyness or anxiety (for which I'm renown), just an inward happyness of having found you. It was as though you were always with us, but had just had a bloody long holiday. In fact 44 years . . .

Now that we have met, I'm reasured to that fact that I have yet another sister to help organise my life . . .

My first impression of Jock and Mandy and Jamie and you was 'what a great family' and throughout that afternoon, this was rectified by the sheer delight, pleasure and excitement radiating on your faces. A day to remember. I will cherish it for ever.

Jean wrote quite frequently as well, often sharing the same letter with Joe. Ron does not seem to have bothered. Pat had never learnt to read or write.

In September Jean wrote to thank Gill for a surprise present. 'Pat and I had to work overtime tonight. We got home at six, cooked ourselves a meal, and were just sitting at the table when there was a knock on the door. A man stood there with a most gorgeous bouquet of flowers. Jill, it was so beautiful, and the words. They sounded so sincere. I wanted to cry. I rushed next door to show them. Then Pat and I went up to the phone box and rang Kath. Thanks Jill. The flowers will die, but the card will outlive me.'

Jean mentions in one of her letters that certain members of the younger generation are still not as excited by what has happened as their parents. 'I think I can understand, but I don't think any of you will regret what you have done.'

In June, Evelyn wrote to say she is now sending letters to various organisations to try to find May and has asked David to contact the National Children's Homes, from where they think he was adopted.

David and Margaret's letters from Hull go over their life so far, about going to Australia, and what they have found out about David's background. In one letter David says that the story about his parents wanting to adopt two of the triplets was probably wrong.

This is just what my mother told me when she told me I was adopted. I'm afraid I can't find out anything more as she died in 1961. I was asking Dad about it the other week. He said Mam did most of the letter writing to the adoption society. He said the only reason they picked me was that there were two of us sat on a bed. I had got up, picked up a doll, and had run across the floor and had said 'Hello Mummy' to my father. He didn't even know I had been one of triplets.

Every so often, my parents would send a donation and a photo to the adoption society until I was 21. If the people who adopted May had to let the adoption people know how she was going on, they might be able to let us know something. What do you think, Jill?

In another letter David says that eighteen years earlier he had contacted the Salvation Army for help in finding his sisters. 'They put us off and said we might cause family problems. I suppose we will all eventually meet up in the end.'

Margaret writes in one letter to Evelyn that they have had a reply from the National Children's Homes in London: 'They looked into all their files and they haven't found him [David], but they kindly sent two more addresses of children's homes which sound similar, so we are going to try them.'

They all sent photographs to each other, of themselves and their families, and noted any comparisons. The two brothers, Ron and Joe, look very similar — chubby-faced and cheerful — but it's hard to see any family resemblance between them and David, their triplet brother. He is smaller, thin-faced and has a receding hairline. Perhaps he is more like their father Wills than his brothers.

There were stronger resemblances between the girls, so they all seemed to think, in character and looks. From their photographs at the time, Gill does look very like Jean and Pat.

★ ★ ★

It is clear that the big reunion had been a huge success for the whole family, that they all genuinely felt the ties of blood emerging and strengthening. David and Gill had found seven of their eight brothers and sisters still alive, which is quite remarkable, especially since Pat and Evelyn had both always suffered health problems. But they all realised that there was the possibility that the missing final triplet had not been quite so lucky. None the less, the search for May went on. Evelyn and Margaret continued to write endless letters to magazines and radio programmes whenever the subject of adoption came up.

16

Adoption from the Seventies

The 1976 Adoption Act got a lot of attention, before and after it was passed. The media latched on to the romance of family reunions with long-lost relatives and, conversely, the universal fear of a knock on the door from someone in one's past who is unwelcome in the present. However far fewer people than expected did decide to take advantage of the change in the law. It was estimated that in 1976 there were 600,000 adopted people in England and Wales over the age of eighteen who now had legal access to their adoption details; only fifteen per cent of them came forward in the sixteen years after the Act was passed.

This might suggest that most adoptees are not bursting with a desire to find out about their birth family, or possibly that they don't want to know out of respect for their adopted parents. Or it may just have been that many were not aware of the change in the law.

Twice as many females as males came forward. The significance of this is a matter of conjecture. Women carry and give birth to their children, so perhaps they have more interest in their own birth mothers. Pregnancy is very often the trigger that prompts adopted women to start investigating their own birth, though not in the case of our triplets. Gill and Helena, on becoming mothers, still had no desire to trace their own birth family.

Another possible explanation is that women seem to have higher levels of interest and sensitivity towards relationships and family affairs. Men are often less driven to get to the roots of such matters, are more willing to suppress any interest in them.

Whatever their reasons, the relatively small proportion who did come forward was enough to provide a decent set of examples which could be analysed. Historically one of the problems with adoption is that few reliable surveys could be done on the subject because of the inbuilt secrecy surrounding it. In the years after 1976 various psychologists and academics tried to get to grips with the raw material now available to them. Details of adoptees applying for their birth certificates were recorded; sample groups were approached and asked about their personal experiences of adoption.

Some of the surveys were based on pretty small samples, but overall they revealed that up to eighty per cent considered they'd had 'good' adoptions, while around twenty per cent said their experiences had been poor. Half had not learned about their adoption until they were over the age of five; a third had not been told until they were at least ten or older. About twenty per cent had not been told, or did not find out until they were teenagers or adults. Being told when they were teenagers appeared to be the most distressing time.

According to the 1970s studies, the vast majority of adopted adults were leading happy, well-adjusted lives. One or two surveys seemed to show there were slightly more referrals to psychologists amongst adopted children than birth children, but this was probably inevitable. Adoptive parents tend to care more, which can lead to overreacting to what is probably normal behaviour in any child as he or she grows up. As adults, while many of those who had been adopted were curious, and some showed a psychological need to know something about their original background, most did not actively want to meet either of their birth parents. Over half of those applying for their birth certificates said they merely wanted the information. About thirty per cent intended to trace their birth parents; only twenty per cent wanted to go and meet them.

One survey suggested that the latter were comprised of three groups: those whose parents had given them a reasonable explanation of their origins; those whose childhood and teenage years at home had been unhappy or unsettled; and those who had just gone through a major personal crisis in their own lives. However, later studies in the 1980s suggested that the only real common link amongst those wanting to meet their birth mother was simple curiosity.

★ ★ ★

After 1976 adoption as experienced by our triplets more or less came to an end.

Adoption figures began to drop dramatically from their peak in 1968, when there were 28,000 adoptions in England and Wales, to 10,240 — less than half — in 1982. In 1995, the figure fell further to only 4100 and this included a great many older children, adopted over the age of ten from institutions, fostering, or care of some sort. Today it is estimated that only around two hundred babies, aged two years and under, are adopted each year in England and Wales. Nothing, really, compared with the good old, bad old days.

For many social, economic and political reasons, adoption is no longer about purely British-born babies being sent off to live with total strangers, having been cut off completely from their birth families, and the supply of such babies has dried up, though the demand is still there.

There are two main reasons for this. Firstly, since the 1960s, the general availability and acceptance of reliable contraception methods have made the birth of unplanned, unwanted babies less likely. Secondly, the social stigma of being an unmarried mother has gone. Nowadays unmarried women have babies willingly and deliberately — a concept that would amaze and appal our Victorian ancestors. Even if a young woman has been seduced by a bounder, been taken advantage of by the boss of her office, or just had too much to drink and can't quite remember how she conceived, she will not be cast out from society. Her life will not be ruined, she will not be forced to feel shame and disgrace. Should she *not* want to have the baby she has the choice of the morning-after pill, or she can have an abortion by walking into a clinic off the street — a high street, not a back street.

Society will in fact encourage her, or at least enable her, to go ahead and have the child on her own. Side by side with changing social and moral attitudes since the 1960s have come much government and local council legislation. There are now facilities for the unmarried mother, and financial help and housing benefits which will assist her, should she choose to bring up her child on her own. She has rights and powers she never had before. And the bounder won't get away with it as he might have done in the past. The father as well as the state has to contribute to the child's upbringing. Unfairness and inequalities remain, but compared with social attitudes and legal provisions for a single mother just forty years ago, things are dramatically different.

In addition, the present wisdom is that unless there is an obvious reason why a birth mother is incapable, because of drugs or mental problems, for example, it will always be better for a child to be with her than in care. Hence there are only a few hundred babies available for adoption each year.

The major care problems with children today centre not on getting babies adopted, but on what to do with older children when they are considered to be in need of care. Because of the increase in marital breakdown, divorce,

144

unmarried partners, continuing inner-city poverty, drug and alcohol abuse, or single mothers finding that they simply can't cope, there has been an increase in older children, damaged or rejected for a variety of reasons, being taken into care.

Care institutions themselves have come in for a great deal of criticism. Not just because of the many, well-publicised scandals and court cases involving sexual or physical abuse in such places, but because keeping children in an institution might in theory be better than leaving them with bad mothers or useless dads, but in practice it is far from satisfactory.

There are today 58,000 children of all ages in council care in England, sixty-seven per cent of whom have mental health problems of some sort. Around seventy per cent will leave their institution at the age of sixteen and go out into the world with no qualifications whatsoever.

A hundred years ago children in need tended to be much as Dr Barnardo had found them — toddlers abandoned by their mothers, left to survive in the street, begging, thieving or just starving. Adoption was one solution to this.

Today, children in need tend to be much older, damaged in some way by society or by their parents and stuck in institutions that appear to be doing them little good. Could adoption, which at one time seemed to be out of fashion, or at least fading out, be one of the solutions?

While the surveys and analyses of children in care have revealed what the problems are and how poor their life chances are, research in recent years into adoption has pointed to its merits and advantages.

Almost every survey on adoption indicates that adopted children do no worse in life than birth children. If anything, the signs are that they do better. In 1958 the National Child Development Study was set up to monitor the progress and development of all children born in England, Scotland and Wales in the first week of March 1958. In 1972 an initial report looked at the progress of adopted children at the age of seven. It showed them making excellent progress on a broad range of educational and social measures, ahead in many respects of children being brought up by their real parents. A subsequent study in 1980 suggested that it wasn't the simple fact of being adopted that enhanced their chances, but the fact that adoptive parents are a self-selected group who have better housing, more money, happier marriages and more stable backgrounds than poor and deprived single mothers coping on their own. Later studies seem to show that as adopted children grow up, the differences and benefits even out.

As for nurture versus nature, you can change your social class when you get adopted, moving up or down the social scale depending on your new parents, but there is little evidence that adoptees grow up to be more intelligent if their adopted parents are more intelligent than their birth parents. In fact a survey in 1975 on intelligence indicated that the IQ of adopted children corresponded more closely to that of their biological parents than their adopted parents.

It is of course very hard to compute, compare and contrast all the advantages of adoption, but almost everyone now agrees that it is on the whole a good thing, for the individual and for society.

In the 1990s adoption came back into the public arena. Of course, adoption happens to be very cheap for the government. In fact it costs nothing, since adopting parents, as opposed to fostering parents, normally receive no state benefits other than the allowances they would get for bringing up their own birth children. The government began the long process of creating a new Adoption Act that would incorporate and reflect the latest systems and wisdoms. Various pressure groups started pushing for their ideas, knowledge and expertise to be incorporated into whatever new rules might come into operation, and it was, in the end, one of these little support groups working in the field of adoption that helped to bring our triplets together.

The 1976 Adoption Act had helped the triplets by bringing the subject into the open and enabling David to access his birth certificate. Although the Act enabled an adopted person over the age of eighteen to have access to their adoption details, it didn't enable a mother whose child had been adopted to find out what had happened to that child, nor — more crucially for the triplets — did it help siblings to find out about one another.

Therefore, the appearance of such support groups was to prove pivotal in Gill and David's search for their third triplet. Not that they were aware of such groups. Neither had they been following all the changes going on in the field. They were still hoping that one day, one year, one decade, contact might be made with the missing third triplet by writing enough letters and phoning enough radio programmes. If, of course, the third triplet was still alive, and if she was willing to be contacted.

Kate Woolway (later
Hodder), mother of the
triplets, aged about
eighteen

Florrie Woolway, Kate's
younger sister, aged three

Wills Hodder, father
of the triplets, aged
thirty-four

Wills' marriage to Kate, October 1919, at St Lawrence church in Seal Chart. Right of the bride, seated, are her parents Fred and Eliza Woolway. Behind the groom, with pipe, is his father Ephraim; seated, with stick, is his grandfather – also Ephraim. Florrie is their bridesmaid.

Four generations of Hodders, 1920. *Left to right*: Wills and Ron; Wills' grandfather Ephraim; Wills' father Ephraim

Kate with Ron, the first of her nine children

The oldest three of the nine Hodder children: Evelyn, Ron and Kath, 1928

Evelyn, Joe, Kath and Ron, 1934, having been taken into Dr Barnardo's care after the death of their mother. This is their official admission photograph.

Thomas Barnardo

Thomas and Syrie Barnardo with their daughter Marjori

Dr Barnardo's head
office in Stepney
Causeway

An example of Thomas Barnardo's controversial 'before
nd after' photography of waifs for his first home for boys

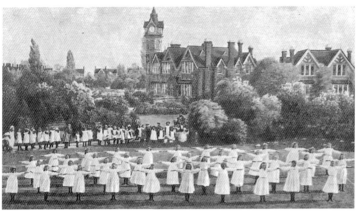

Musical dri
at the Girls
Village
Home,
Barkingside
Essex – hor
to Evelyn a
Kath

A fête at the
Girls' Village
Home,
1930s

The Boys'
Garden
Centre –
home to Ro
and Joe

Evelyn Hodder in her
Land Army uniform

Evelyn Hodder, aged
sixteen. She and Kath both
went into service on leaving
Dr Barnardo's.

Kath Hodder in her
WRAF uniform

Jean Hodder, who was brought up in Stone Street with her sister Pat at Post Office House – their grandparents' house

Jean and Pat apple picking

Post Office House, Stone Street

Emily Davey with her newly adopted daughter, Gill – the first of the triplets to be adopted

Gill, aged four, at Rock House in Lynmouth, Devon, where her new family ran a guest house

Gill, aged fourteen, dressed as a Tyrollean dancer

Gill, aged fifteen

Gill and Jock's
wedding, 1954

The Manse, Barnet. Mabel, the maid who was cruel to Helena, lived in the top attic room.

Reverend Thomas and Jeanie's wedding, 1921. They adopted Helena in 1934.

Helena, aged three and Pam, aged five

Helena, in the back row, fourth from the left, having been ordained as a sister for the National Children's Homes, 1954

Helena and Harry's wedding, 1960. Reverend Thomas and his wife are on the right at the back.

Helena and Harry with their children Maryon, Collette and Stanley, 1967. Note Helena's resemblance to her birth mother Kate.

David, aged about two, in what is probably his official adoption photograph

David, aged three, having been adopted by Walter and Ivy Welburn, who had a grocer's shop in Beverley, Yorkshire

Ivy Welburn

David, aged twelve, in the
Church Lads' Brigade

David, aged twenty-two,
when he was doing his
National Service

David and Margaret's wedding, 1958. Walter and Ivy
are to the left of David.

Evelyn Hodder,
1976, just after
she had helped
to track down
and unite
David and Gill

Pam Hodgkins, founder of NORCAP

Gill, David and Helena with Gloria Hunniford, after the triplet were finally reunited in 2001

The grave of Kate and Wills Hodder. The date of death given for Kate is wrong, in fact she died on 19 May, the day after giving birth to the triplets.

The triplets' seventieth birthday party, 2002

17

The Triplets in the Eighties

Helena continued to live in Kent as her children grew up and got married, with no interest whatsoever in knowing anything about her birth family and completely unaware that her triplet brother and sister and older siblings were trying to track her down.

She remained devoted to her adopted parents all their lives. Her mother died in 1963, at which point her father returned to London and took up a semi-retired position in a church in Stoke Newington, to be near Helena and her family. He died in 1981 in Hackney hospital aged ninety-two. But not even the death of both her adopted parents sparked off any desire in Helena to know about her real parents.

Despite his haemophilia Helena's husband Harry managed to carry on working until 1988, when he retired aged fifty-six. He had continued to have constant blood transfusions and in 1987 had become infected with the HIV virus. There was then a further disaster when a locum surgeon, unaware of his condition, did not administer the anti-haemophilia factor during an operation. Harry died in hospital in 1988, so very soon after he had retired. In the end, the family sued the hospital for negligence and did receive some out-of-court compensation.

Four weeks before he died Collette, Harry and Helena's second daughter, gave birth to her second child Matthew, who was also found to be suffering from haemophilia. Fortunately, there has been great progress since Harry was young and today injections can mostly control it, so there is not the same need for constant blood transfusions.

In 1989 Helena moved from their Maidstone house to Dartford, to be nearer her two daughters. Maryon, her oldest child, married Howard and they went on to have three children; Collette, Helena's younger daughter, married Charles and they also had three children, Samantha, Matthew and Chris. Helena's son, Stanley, married Sarah and they had two children. Helena kept in regular touch with all three of her children and her eight grandchildren. She had become a member of the local Church of England (there was no Congregational church nearby) and she was active in the Mothers' Union and various other local organisations and charities. From 1994 to 1996 she was also President of the Wilmington branch of the Women's Institute. While not at meetings or with her family, she did a lot of knitting and embroidery.

Living in her bungalow with her was Pamela — the sister she had grown up with, the baby girl whom Reverend Thomas and his wife had adopted before they had adopted Helena. Pamela never married. After secretarial work in London she went off to Kenya and Uganda for several years and worked there for the government. When she came back to London she worked in the travel trade for some time, and her father came to live with her when he was widowed. When Helena's husband Harry died Pamela moved in with Helena.

They have always got on very well and are as close as birth sisters, though Pamela has a rather posher voice. 'You mean plummy,' she says, laughing. Her years with the white settlers in Africa probably enhanced her rather pre-war accent. Helena's work in children's homes and her life in Hackney have softened her vowels over the years and she has no accent, as such, just standard London-educated English.

Their house is nicely cluttered, full of ornaments, books and examples of Helena's handicrafts. She paid £140,000 for the bungalow when she bought it in 1989. It is now worth about three times as much. All house prices in London's commuter belt have soared in recent years, but theirs increased more than many others because of the construction only a few miles away of the massive Bluewater shopping complex. There is also building work going on nearby for a new Channel Tunnel station. Both have conspired to make Helena's particular neighbourhood rather desirable.

Wilmington is a very attractive village anyway, far more so than Dartford, which seems a pretty soulless town. I arrived at its railway station and followed signposts to the Tourist Office, only to find it had long since been closed.

'Yes, Dartford is a bit messy,' says Helena. 'We've lost Marks & Spencer and Woolworths and several other big shops since Bluewater opened. Only the Co-op is left, plus a lot of charity shops. But here in Wilmington it is very nice. We've still got fields and horses around us.'

Wilmington's main claim to fame in recent history is that it was the home of Mick Jagger, who grew up there and went on to Dartford Grammar School. Today there is a Mick Jagger Centre in Dartford beside the school, where concerts are held.

★   ★   ★

Gillian and Jock left Lynton and Lynmouth in 1981, which was a bit of a wrench after so many years as part of the community. But Jock had been offered a promotion by the Post Office, which meant moving to Barnstaple, where he became an inspector, a job he held until he retired in 1995, aged sixty-five.

They bought quite a large house in Barnstaple, which looks very like a guest house with its knick-knacks and ornaments and air of ordered tidiness. David and Gill's Hodder relations continued to visit them there on their holidays. Mandy, their daughter, was living not too far away in Somerset. She had become a care worker, looking after children with disabilities. She had got married to David and had one daughter, Frances. Jamie, their adopted son, was also living locally. He was married with a daughter, Savana, but the marriage eventually collapsed.

Gill often wondered if they would ever make

contact with the missing triplet, but didn't do much about it. She left it to Evelyn in Harrow or Margaret in Beverley to keep writing letters to likely agencies.

However, in 1999 she was listening to Radio Devon one day when she heard a programme about missing relatives. She rang in, saying she was looking for her third triplet. She mentioned a family rumour, which she had picked up from the Hodders, that May had been adopted by a rich farming family in Somerset. This led to a call from Radio Bristol. 'They then got a phone call from a man who said he had gone to school in Somerset with a May Hodder,' says Gill. 'She had a sister, also adopted, by a local farmer. She had sort of reddish hair. He remembers cycling to school with her every day for a few years. We all got very excited. They made enquiries, and went to see this man. But it was a red herring. It wasn't the same May Hodder.

'I decided after that, that if May was still alive, which was doubtful, she probably didn't want to be tracked down. I personally believed she had emigrated and was now on the other side of the world, impossible to locate.

'I also began to feel that even if we did somehow manage to track her down, I wouldn't be able to cope. It had been exhausting enough twenty-three years earlier when I'd met up with David and my other brothers and sisters, and I'd been a lot younger then. I just didn't have the energy or the interest any more in getting involved with a lot of new people and new relationships.

'I also worried that it might end unhappily. I'd been pleased to meet up with David and the others and didn't regret it, though there had been a few tensions with one person, which I found a bit of a strain. But that had settled down. I just thought that next time, if there was a next time, we might not be so lucky.'

★   ★   ★

Meanwhile, up in Beverley David's wife Margaret continued to make enquiries about her husband's missing triplet sister. But with no success. The problem was getting access to the court's records of May's adoption details. Under the 1976 Act, only the person him-or herself had a legal right to these — there was still no provision for siblings to get details of each other. Margaret did not even know where or at which court the adoption had taken place, which might have been a start in making some local searches.

Adoption agencies who have handled the original adoption are often able and willing to let direct family members have some details from their files, especially when the case has happened many years earlier. But Helena's records were held by the National Children's Adoption Society, which had ceased to exist. The files had been transferred to Westminster City Council but when Margaret wrote to them, she was told they had been lost.

David and Margaret's children grew up and got married. Kevin, Margaret's first child, who had been adopted by David, married Sharron not long after he had returned from Australia. Elizabeth became a nurse and married a policeman with whom she had two children. John became a tattooist in Hull.

David and Margaret continued to be active members of the Church of the Latter-Day Saints. David became an official in their local church — secretary to the leader — which meant attending a meeting once a week, as well as church services. Of their three children only Elizabeth remained a member of the Church after marriage.

In 1989 David took voluntary redundancy from British Aerospace, aged fifty-seven. 'I got a lump sum of £33,000 and a monthly pension of £120. It was the best day's work I'd ever done.'

With the money, they paid off their mortgage and moved around for several years, as they had done during most of their married life, until they returned to Beverley in 1993 and bought a two-bedroom bungalow there. Two years later they bought a ground-floor flat for £37,500 in a new development near the Minster. They paid cash — there was no need for a mortgage this time. 'Margaret wanted to be on the posh side of town for once,' says David.

'One day at the end of 1992, Margaret asked me to feel her breast,' David remembers. 'She thought she had a lump in it. I couldn't feel anything, but perhaps I wasn't feeling it hard enough.

'It was December time, just before Christmas. The doctor's surgery was closed, so she didn't get round to going for a check-up until about a week after Christmas. When she saw the doctor she was rushed straight to hospital, where she was given a mastectomy. She was so worried about what I would think of her. She said she dreaded me seeing what had happened to her. But when I did, I thought they'd made a lovely job. The stitching was really well done.

'When she'd recovered, she was really positive. She took it in her stride and for the next four years life went on as normal. We hardly mentioned it. But in 1997 the cancer came back. It just suddenly took hold of her again. And that was it. She died in a few months.'

Margaret, who had first started the search for the missing triplets, who had always been the one most interested in David's family background, had died without ever knowing the end of the story.

★   ★   ★

Evelyn Hodder, who had of course been equally active in trying to trace May, died in 1996, aged seventy-four. Her younger sister, Kath, the only one who had married, died in 1995 aged seventy-two, and Jean, the pretty one, passed away in 1989. Of the two Hodder brothers who had been in Dr Barnardo's, Ron died in 1994 and Joe in 1997. By the year 2000, therefore, only Pat was alive out of the six older Hodder children — Pat, the most sickly of the Hodders, who had epilepsy and whom their father had asked the rest of his children to look after.

After Margaret and Evelyn died, the documents and details they had collected, the lists of places and organisations they had tried in order to trace the missing triplet, were passed on to Gill and David.

This was one of the reasons Gill had contacted Radio Devon in 1999 — she felt she owed it to their memory to do her bit. When that had not led anywhere she had as good as given up wondering whether news of their third triplet would ever come to light.

However, the local Devon programme had been part of a national project called *Search* and unbeknown to Gill and David the producer, Nick Handel, became very interested in tracking down the missing triplet.

Back in 1976 adoption stories had been in the news, on the radio and in magazines because adoption reunions had become more common after the change in the law. By the year 2000, when email and the internet had become almost ubiquitous as instant means of communication, there was a growing interest in all sorts of reunions. People wanted to get in touch with old friends with whom they had once been to school or worked. In almost every local newspaper there were stories of old school reunions, or calls for those who had been in a certain class at a certain time to come forward; 'Friends Reunited', a special website created purely for old school friends, began to have millions of hits.

Programmes like *Search* cleverly exploited and took full advantage of this renewed interest in reviving contact with people from one's past, just as radio programmes such as Charlie Chester's had done in the 1970s, giving out regular information about people wanting to meet old friends. But the scale of *Search*, which combined national TV and BBC local radio stations, was much bigger and broader than anything that had ever been done before.

Nick Handel decided to call in the help of a specialist agency, NORCAP — the National Organisation for Counselling Adoptees and Parents — to see if they could provide professional expertise in getting to the bottom of what had happened to the missing triplet. Margaret, David and Evelyn had after all been only amateur sleuths with no experience, knowledge or training in how adoption agencies were organised; the role of social workers; how to deal with local councils; what the law does and does not dictate; what can and cannot be found out and most of all how to overcome seemingly insurmountable obstacles in your path on such searches.

And so into the tale of the triplets entered Pam Hodgkins, the founder of NORCAP.

18

Pam's Story

Pam Hodgkins was herself adopted. Being adopted is very often a reason why people go on to adopt a child themselves, or become involved in some sort of adoption work. Pam's involvement began relatively late in life, when she began to strongly feel that there was a job to be done, a gap to be filled, a need to be catered for. This turned out to be very fortunate for our triplets.

Pam was born in 1952 in Malden, Essex, and was placed for adoption when she was only ten days old. Her adopted parents told her at an early age that she was adopted, so she always knew the truth, or at least as much of it as they knew. Over the years she had acquired a few basic facts about her background. Her mother, Mary, came from the north and had been a drama student, as had her father, Roy. When Mary became pregnant she was in no position to bring up a child and the stigma of a single girl having a baby was still prevalent in 1950s' British society. So it had been planned from the outset that her baby would be adopted.

Her background had been middle class, so the family had whisked her away to a place where she was unknown, which happened to be a village in Essex. The connection was through a local vicar who had been a friend of Mary's family while still a curate. Mary had come to live with him, ostensibly to help with his family, but mainly to have the baby well away from her own family and neighbours. The vicar gave her a temporary home and quite a few sermons about her wicked ways.

After Pam's birth, the vicar and a local doctor arranged for her to be adopted privately, without the involvement of an adoption agency or the social services. (In the 1950s around one third of adopted babies were still being placed through informal arrangements, often involving a local doctor.) So, at the age of four months, Pam was legally adopted by Ernest Richardson, a foreman in a flour mill, and his wife Dorothy — both stout members of the local Church of England. After her adoption, Pam's mother disappeared, either to her home in the north or to London to her lover.

Ernest and Dorothy had no children of their own. When they first adopted Pam they were living in a rented cottage with no inside toilet. Later they moved to a council house.

'My first memory is from about the age of four,' Pam says. 'I had just had my adenoids taken out at home by the local doctor. He sat me at the end of the bed and operated there and then.

'When I was about eight my parents arranged to adopt a little boy. It was all worked out and they even bought the pram. I remember pushing it home from the shop. But it never happened. I think at the last moment the mother decided to keep her baby after all.'

160

Pam didn't mind. She was content as an only child, and happy to be adopted. 'I was proud of it. If anyone at school thought they were getting at me by jeering at me for being adopted, I would say, 'I'm the lucky one. My parents chose me. Your parents had to take what they got — and they now probably wish they hadn't.'

'My parents honestly did say they were lucky to have me. They put me on a pedestal. They were strict when they had to be, but they were totally loving.

'I know now that adopted children often sense something missing, a feeling of not truly belonging, not having a real identity with the family around them. That's the reason why some adopted boys commit suicide as teenagers. Luckily I didn't feel any of this. I was always very happy and secure as a child.

'The trouble only began when I was about fourteen. I had gone to grammar school, one of the first in their family who had ever done so, and I began to feel a bit intellectually superior to my mother. Not to my father. He was uneducated, but he was an intelligent man who could have done much better in life if he had had the opportunities.

'The school disco was coming up and I wanted to stay until it finished at 10.30 p.m. My mother said no, she would pick me up at 9.45. I said it wasn't fair. We had a row, and I shouted at her, 'My real mother would let me out until late!' Then I stormed out.'

Pam went to the local library and found the phone number for the town hall in the town where her mother had originally come from. She had recently learned, through a local doctor who had helped with her adoption, that her mother had gone on to have two children and had been her town's mayoress for a period. She rang the town hall and said she wanted to track down an old friend she'd lost contact with: her name was Mary, she had two children and had been mayoress of the town. That was the sum of her information at the time. Fortunately someone sympathetic answered her call and told Pam the names of the present mayor and mayoress. They didn't fit the bill, but Pam persuaded her to ask one of her colleagues for the names of the last few mayors. None had a wife called Mary either. So Pam hung up and forgot all about her birth mother for the next seventeen years. She had in fact been quite close: her mother had been mayoress just a year earlier than Pam had inquired about. As for the disco, she did go, and kept her mother waiting outside until 10.15.

Pam got decent O levels but refused to go into the sixth form because she wanted to start work. She became a laboratory technician, but decided after two years that it had been a mistake and took up an evening course at college to do A levels. She then applied for a place at teachers' training college.

While waiting for the bus one day she met John Hodgkins, who had been at grammar school with her, though they had never been close friends. They got married a year later, in 1971. She never got to training college: their sons, Neil and Peter, were born in 1974 and 1979, and in 1988 they had a third child, a daughter — Emma.

In 1981 Pam — by nature well organised, some might even say bossy — helped to organise a street party for the wedding of the Prince and Princess of Wales. During the party she got what she thought was an insect bite on her leg and the next day it began to swell up. She saw a doctor, who said she must have a chest X-ray, which didn't seem to make sense — Pam thought she'd just had a gnat bite during the street party. However, having had the X-ray, it turned out that she had a rare condition linked to TB. During subsequent tests and treatment she was constantly asked if there was a history of TB in her family. She didn't know, of course.

It was this incident, at the age of thirty, that convinced her she must make contact with her birth mother, just as Elspeth's diagnosis of diabetes had convinced her.

Pam obtained a copy of her birth certificate, easy to do since she had basic information about her birth mother. This gave her mother's home address. She then bought a map of the town and noticed that at the end of the street where her mother had lived there was a police station. Pam rang the station, gave a policeman the address and said she wanted to make contact with the woman who lived there. The policeman didn't know the woman, but he said he would ask a colleague who had lived locally for years about her.

He rang back to say he had located the

woman. He couldn't give out her new address, but he would ring her and pass on Pam's name and number.

Later that evening Pam's phone rang. It was Mary, her mother, asking what Pam wanted. 'I could sense from her voice she realised who I was,' recalls Pam. 'But she said very little, sounding cold and remote. I just gabbled away non-stop, as I do when I'm nervous. She said it was inconvenient to talk now, but she would ring me later.

'To me, 'later' means later that evening, or a few days later. After a week of silence I realised that what she meant was 'later in my life, sometime before I die'. I wasn't having that. I thought, I'm not letting her ignore me. I can be very headstrong.'

Pam still didn't have her mother's present address, so she rang the police station again, who were surprised to be asked about the same person twice in a week. She managed to extract from them Mary's surname and the fact that her mother was working as a teacher. With all this information, Pam was able to get a copy of her mother's birth certificate, as well as those of Mary's two other children.

Pam then booked a weekend break near the town where her mother was living. She planned to go to Mary's house on the Friday afternoon, reckoning that she would have returned from school by then and would be on her own for some time before the rest of her family came home. She'd written down the vital questions she wanted to ask her mother, mainly about

164

health, on a clipboard. She walked up the drive to the front door, only to hear a man and a woman inside shouting at each other. She seemed to have arrived in the middle of a row. So she went back to her car and waited. Eventually, an elderly man left the house, but someone else arrived immediately. Pam didn't want to doorstep Mary when other people were around in case her existence was still a secret, so she went to a phone box and rang the house. Mary answered. Pam said she needed to see her. Mary said it wasn't convenient. Pam said she was here, outside, in the phone box. She could either pitch up at the house, or meet her later at the hotel where she was staying. Mary agreed to come to Pam's hotel at 6.30, but not for long.

Pam returned to the hotel and waited in her room. At 6.50 Mary had still not turned up and Pam was beginning to accept she may not, when there was a knock on her door.

'When I opened the door, my mother was standing there. She put her arms round me and hugged me. It was the single most stunning moment in my life.'

They talked emotionally for three hours. Mary explained that she had been having a relationship with her boyfriend, Roy, dating back to their days together at drama school. They had then lived together in London. When Mary went home to her family for Christmas in 1950 she feared she was pregnant and she wrote to Roy. In his letter back he never mentioned the pregnancy, he just asked her for money as their rent was due. Mary was so furious and upset by

165

this that she decided to have nothing to do with him again. So her own father had never known about Pamela.

Some years later, when she was about to get married, Mary confessed to her husband-to-be that she had had a baby. He said he could accept this. But she had never told her own children.

After that initial meeting Pam met her mother quite regularly, although never at her mother's home. She also wrote to Mary at her school. One day her daughter happened to look in her mother's school-bag for something and she found one of Pam's letters. She confronted her mother and Mary had to confess. Pam was then summoned by Mary's husband to meet the whole family at last.

Having been accepted by her birth mother, Pam decided to track down her father. Mary had had no contact with Roy Hodges since that Christmas of 1950, but she had seen his photograph in a newspaper. In 1957 he had married another actress who had gone on to achieve rather more success than he or Mary: the Oscar-winning star, Glenda Jackson.

Pam looked her up in *Who's Who* and found her agent's address, to which she sent a letter for Ms Jackson. In it she explained the reasons for her wish to be put in contact with Roy Hodges. By this time Glenda and Roy's marriage had ended, but the information must have been passed on because one Saturday evening Pam got a phone call from Roy. 'I'm not sure how to put this,' he said, 'but I think I must be your father.'

Pam met up with him and heard his side of the story of her birth. 'Roy agreed that my mother did write to him saying she might be pregnant. But when she never wrote again he assumed it had been a false alarm and he went on with his life,' she says.

Roy Hodges and Glenda Jackson had one son, Daniel, who was fourteen when Pam came into their lives — another blood relative about whom she had never known. Pam and her family got on well with Daniel. He went on holiday with them and Pam was with him after a tragic event in 1992 in a pub when Daniel lost the sight of one eye trying to break up a fight.

'Daniel and I share the same sense of humour,' says Pam. 'But I'm not so close with my mother's children. The closest family I have gained are my mother and my brother Peter, who recently emigrated to Canada. He and his family have welcomed me with open arms.'

Mary died of breast cancer in 1995. Pam was greatly saddened, but it was a comfort to have the peace of mind of knowing that she had traced her mother in time to forge a close friendship with her, to find out about her background, and to understand fully the reasons for her adoption.

Pam showed great determination in tracking down Mary, using guile and basic common sense to do so. She didn't know it at the time, but these skills would come in very useful again in her future.

19

Pam Founds NORCAP

While Pam Hodgkins was searching for her mother, she was also taking care of her own family and building a career for herself. When her sons were old enough to go to school, she took a course at her local technical college to learn to teach health awareness. Having completed it, she found herself teaching apprentice plumbers and carpenters communication skills. She so enjoyed teaching that she then did a two-year PGCE and got a teaching certificate.

In 1982 she was returning from London on a train when she happened to pick up a discarded copy of the *Daily Express*, a paper she never usually read. On the letters page was correspondence from a lady called Heather, who wanted to find her birth mother. Some readers were against her trying to do so, others were for it.

Pam had just successfully made contact with her own mother and was still in the white heat of the new relationship. So there and then she scribbled a letter to the *Daily Express*, pointing out that under the law anyone over eighteen years of age had a right to their birth certificate. She added that it was not necessarily all that difficult to track people down, that she had done it and the result had been more emotional than she had expected but very rewarding. She finished by saying that if Heather wanted to contact her for help she could do so. She gave her address, signed and posted the letter, then forgot about it.

Ten days later the postman arrived and asked where she wanted her sack put. She didn't know what he meant, until he showed her a sack full of letters — all for her. The *Daily Express* had published Pam's scribbled note without her realising it and sixty-five people had replied to her.

Pam was sure that if there were so many people out there wanting to trace their birth mother, there must be an organisation to help them. She rang her local social services department. She was passed through various offices, and eventually put through to the assistant director for Warwickshire social services. She was most interested to hear about Pam's letters, but couldn't help deal with them, or redirect them. She told Pam there had been an organisation called Jigsaw which worked in this field, but it appeared to have closed. She suggested contacting an umbrella group called the British Agencies for Adoption and Fostering. But, she advised — only half joking — the best thing to do was obvious — begin her own support group.

Pam had not thought of this, but the more she did, the more appealing it sounded. Back in her village, she contacted some local friends from various coffee mornings and they all sat down and began to answer the sixty-five letters as best they could, working out a standard response

169

which they typed out and copied.

The completion of this, they decided, counted as the beginnings of a support group, so they contacted their local newspapers, who published a few stories about their group. These got them some publicity, but didn't actually bring in any offers of help. All the same, they decided to formalise their group and call it, ambitiously, the National Organisation for Counselling Adoptees and Parents, or NORCAP for short.

Members were charged £2 a year to join. It was run by volunteers from the local community, who helped in their spare time by giving out information such as how to get hold of birth records, simple advice on the law and general support for adults affected in some way by adoption.

By the end of the first year they had about one hundred members — most of whom had come from the original sixty-five letter-writers.

They had also started a register in an out-of-date desk diary, in which they recorded the basic personal details of every member trying to trace someone. Around twenty per cent of their members were birth mothers wanting to contact a child they had put out for adoption years previously. The rest were mainly people who had been adopted, or relatives of people who had been adopted, wanting to contact the birth family. In the register the name of the adoptee was written in blue on the page of his or her birthday, and the name of the person searching was written in red beside the name and date of birth of the person for whom they were looking. The names would very rarely tie up, as almost everybody's adopted name changes, but eventually the birth dates might connect two people looking for each other. That was the theory.

By 1984 Pam had qualified as a further education teacher and got herself a full-time job. She could no longer cope with running NORCAP from her kitchen table, not having the time or the space for all the paperwork that had accumulated.

The organisation had had two annual meetings by then, the first in Coventry Cathedral and the second in London. The first meeting had brought forward a woman called Linda Savell who had had to retire from work due to her ill health. She was housebound, but nonetheless had the energy, skills and enthusiasm needed to take over the reins of NORCAP. So control of the organisation was handed over and all its records and papers were moved from Pam's kitchen to Linda's spare room.

As NORCAP continued to grow, they needed more space. A religious charity just three miles from Linda's home offered them the use of a room for nothing, and Linda was able to run the operation from there with low overheads and local volunteers. Pam contributed help on the phone for two hours most evenings.

By this time NORCAP had managed to set up and train local leaders in different parts of the country, mostly people who had themselves traced relatives. They were all still volunteers, working from their own kitchen tables — all amateurs without trained social workers or allied professionals working with them.

NORCAP continued this way for two more years, as Pam tried to make contacts on a national level and get the social-work hierarchy and government departments to take her seriously.

'For the first two years NORCAP was treated rather patronisingly,' she says. 'Even when we did begin to be recognised, we were still kept at arm's length. Officials didn't seem to want to recommend us. When people approached them about adoption counselling, they would give an official list, then perhaps tack on a mention of 'a woman in Warwickshire, who we don't know much about.' '

Pam did slowly manage to get support from various well-known people in the social-work field who were interested in NORCAP's pioneering work. People like John Stroud, assistant director of social services in Hertford-shire, who had made a speciality of studying adopted twins. He helped them to work out a system for training their contact leaders.

'A big breakthrough came when I was invited, as chairman of NORCAP, to a seminar being held by the Department of Health. I felt at last we had arrived.'

There was another breakthrough in 1986 when a birth parent and an adopted child were brought together by a link in their adoption register — the first reunion it had achieved. Statistically, this should not have happened for another two years.

As they began to achieve more and more successful reunions, they received a Community Care award, which enabled them to give up their written register and invest in a computer database for all their records.

But one of the stumbling blocks towards further progress remained the lack of a qualified social worker. One hundred and forty years earlier Thomas Barnardo had never had to worry about such things. He created his own systems, trained his own staff and made up his own rules. Even forty years before, adoptions had been carried out on a very informal basis: local doctors taking it upon themselves to place children with people they knew, without bothering to inform the social services. But by the 1980s the whole field of adoption was governed by laws and regulations. Strict procedures had to be followed, only properly trained people could do certain things. Such rules persist, of course, protecting vulnerable individuals from unqualified people giving out bad advice which might result in untold damage or trauma. We are also in a world where people are quick to sue if they feel hurt or aggrieved. An organisation like NORCAP, therefore, would be well advised to protect itself with some expert advice and consultation.

There were still no social workers involved in running NORCAP by 1986, so Pam decided to volunteer herself. Her husband, who works in the field of transport, could not afford or be expected to help finance her studies, so she looked around for funding. Eventually she got a bursary from the Department of Health to study to become a social worker at Leicester Polytechnic, now De Montfort University. While there, she was still actively involved in NORCAP's work, going to the Department of Health for conferences, or appearing on television to discuss adoption issues, then returning to Leicester to resume life as an ordinary student.

Towards the end of her two-year course, she found herself pregnant, which had not been planned, and in 1988 Emma was born.

Pam qualified later that year and returned to work full-time for NORCAP whilst Emma was a young baby. However, she began to recognise that there were conflicts of interest in being the founder and an employee of the organisation. So, in 1990 she got a job as a social worker. She now works for the West Midlands Post-Adoption Services and for Oxfordshire social services, whilst remaining involved with NORCAP as its political leader and main activist.

In 1991 the Registrar General's department itself introduced some of the methods that were being used by NORCAP. They now hold an adoption contact register and an adopted person over the age of eighteen can apply to have their name listed on part one of the register, while a relative of someone who has been adopted can apply to be listed on part two. When their details match up the adoptee is informed that someone is trying to trace them. In fact, though, this service has not been widely used, perhaps through lack of publicity.

In 1995 Pam was awarded an MBE in the New Year Honours List in recognition of her services to the world of adoption. She seemed to be permanently rushing around, balancing her jobs, her NORCAP work and her family with endless national and local committees, advice work and writing reports and submissions. No obstacle seems to defeat or deflate her, she sees the broad picture and sweeps on ahead, making contacts and trying her best to influence people. She says she's been lucky in having a supportive husband. Her daughter Emma has only known her as a whirlwind mother, constantly rushing about, but her two older sons often look back rather wistfully to the years when she pottered about at home.

By the year 2000, NORCAP was employing five full-time staff and five volunteers at new offices in Wheatley. They had 50,000 names on their register and had helped reunite 2500 families. They had created a network of trained volunteers in every part of the country who were always available on the telephone and held advice sessions at the Family Records Centre in London, and they had compiled a list of accredited researchers who could be hired to help track down records and certificates.

Perhaps most importantly of all, they had established their own search room at Wheatley, which members could use. Apart from access to their own computerised register they had also acquired access to the Registrar General's index of births, marriages and deaths on microfiche. In under twenty years of existence NORCAP had become an important national organisation, which had helped thousands of men and women and was recognised and trusted by government ministers and local social-work departments. It was still a charity without any core funding, relying on subscriptions and donations from members, but it had managed to gain access to a regular sequence of government funds for special projects.

Pam had created this formidable organisation and so she of all people was well aware in 2000 that law changes were being discussed which could affect NORCAP. She knew from her close involvement with government departments that a new bill on children and adoption was to be debated in the forthcoming year. Naturally, she was hoping that any new law would make NORCAP's job easier and enable them to help even more people. Over the years they had acquired a large number of members desperate to be put in touch with their families, who had been unable, for various reasons, to get their hands on the final missing piece of the jigsaw. People very like our triplets. Thousands of others had discovered that while the 1976 Act had given an adopted person over the age of eighteen the right of access to their own records, it did not allow mothers or siblings similar access. Families separated by adoption were therefore being kept apart, despite desperately seeking each other.

NORCAP saw it as a human right for someone to know if they had a brother or sister. Pam had successfully managed to unite many siblings over the years, but there were also instances where she had failed. Ken from Birmingham was such a case. In 1945, Ken was aged thirteen and was living alone with his mother. His father was in the army, but nothing had been heard of him for some time and he was presumed missing, killed in the war.

One day Ken was called into his mother's bedroom and she thrust a bundle at him. 'Here, get rid of this,' she said. Ken took the bundle to their neighbour, an old woman, who unwrapped it and found inside a newborn baby. They washed it, wrapped it in a blanket and Ken took it back to his mother. 'I said get rid of it,' she said. 'I don't want it.'

Ken took the bundle back to the neighbour and for the next two months they cared for the baby — a little girl whom they called Mavis. Then, out of the blue, a message came from the War Office, saying that Ken's father had been found alive in a POW camp and was now about to come home. His mother collected Mavis and with Ken went to Birmingham town hall, where she handed the baby over for adoption. She swore Ken to secrecy, saying it would kill his father if he ever knew.

Ken told no one, except his own wife when he got married. But in 1996, when his mother died, he finally contacted Pam to help find Mavis. She had been in his mind all his life. Pam tried every agency and all the public records, but failed to locate Mavis.

'I know the adoption records must be in Birmingham, but no one is allowed to see them.

If and when the law changes, I'm sure we'll find Mavis, if she is still alive,' Pam told Ken at the end of her search.

As Pam gleaned snippets about the proposed new bill, she became anxious that it should bring information on adoptions out into the open even further, enable things to go forward not backwards. Otherwise all NORCAP's hard work since 1982 would be wasted. When she heard about the triplets, she felt their story was a perfect example of the problems she was coming up against. It was a more interesting and unusual case than someone like Ken's, and she knew if she succeeded in tracking down the missing triplet, it might well produce some useful publicity for NORCAP. But, far more importantly, she badly wanted to help David and Gill, having travelled along a similar road herself.

20

Bev's Story

Pam had dealt with other cases where multiple-birth siblings had been separated at birth, during her time working for NORCAP. One of these cases concerning a missing twin. It had all begun on her doorstep, in the little Warwickshire village of Hampton Magna. Almost opposite her lived Bev and Geoffrey Claridge, both school teachers with children roughly the same age as Pam's. It turned out that Bev had also been adopted, which helped to strengthen their friendship, but when Pam first started her own search and subsequently began NORCAP, Bev appeared uninterested.

'I remember talking to Bev about what I was going to do, it must have been twenty years ago now, and she seemed to think it wasn't nice, wasn't fair to track down your birth family. So I was very surprised some years later when she rang to tell me what she was now doing.'

Bev, today, admits she might have said such a thing, but it was only to protect her adopted parents. Deep down, she had always been longing to meet her birth mother.

She was born in 1947 and adopted as a baby by a couple in Gloucestershire who had been married for ten years and had no children. During four of those years they had seen nothing of each other as he had been in the war with the RAF.

'When they met again, during Christmas 1945 they were almost strangers to each other. They'd become different people, so it took a while to get back to normal life. Then I think they panicked when a baby didn't come along. They wanted one at once. They went to an adoption agency on Whiteladies Road in Bristol, requesting a boy. They saw one they liked, but he appeared to be with his mother, who was just leaving him. My mother turned around and left. She didn't want to adopt a baby whose mother she had seen. They came back a week later with an appointment to see a girl baby, which was me.'

After about eighteen months Bev's adopted mother became pregnant, as often happens. She had a baby girl, Caroline, a sister for Bev.

'I always knew I was adopted,' says Bev. 'My parents never hid it and always said I was special because they had chosen me, though they didn't seem to know much about my background. I remember in 1976 when the new law came in that gave adopted children access to their own records, my mother was most upset. She didn't want me to try to find my real mother. In the end I had to promise I wouldn't.

'I did get my birth certificate and found that my real name had been Ruth Hetherington. My parents had told me that my mother had been a nurse and that my father had been rich and important. I don't know where they got that from. I didn't really believe it, but I liked to think about it, fantasise what my mother looked like.

But I never for one moment fantasised that I might be a twin.'

Bev went from grammar school to a teachers' training college and married her childhood boyfriend, Geoffrey Claridge, while still at college in 1967. They had two children — Ben, born in 1969 and Amy, in 1971. Geoffrey turned out to be a high-flyer, becoming a headmaster while still in his late twenties.

'The need to find my mother grew stronger as I got older. Each day on my birthday I'd always thought about her. Once I had my own children, my feelings grew more intense. I loved them dearly, so I thought, how awful, how terrible for my mother to have had to give up me. You can't forget about the day you gave birth, so each day on my birthday I knew she must be thinking about me. It got to the stage when I felt I just had to tell her I was OK. That was all. Just reassure her I was fine and had had a happy childhood.

'I had, of course, promised my adopted mother I would never try to make contact. That's probably why I was not keen when Pam started her work. I loved my mother very much, but over the years the emotions within me became more important than my promise. I felt such a need. I had to do something about it.'

In 1993, Bev rang Pam. Bev's father was very ill and her mother still alive, so she had decided not to let either of them know what she was doing.

'I said to Pam, 'You'll never guess, I want to track down my mother.' I'd made a few enquiries already, but got nowhere. I asked Pam what should I do next. I'd got my birth certificate but that's all.'

Pam told her to read out everything it said on the birth certificate, which Bev thought was a bit pointless. After all, she'd read it a thousand times. When she read out, 'Born at 8.30 a.m. on 3 March 1947,' Pam asked her to repeat that bit. Then she told Bev to sit down and pour herself a stiff gin and tonic.

Pam explained that the mention of an exact time meant Bev had been part of a multiple birth. The other baby could have been stillborn, but they needed to get a copy of its birth certificate. When Pam had done so, she found that Bev had a twin brother called Peter, who had been born some hours later. On his birth certificate it said 'adopted'. Pam explained this indicated he had survived to at least nineteen weeks, the youngest age at which a child could be adopted at the time. He had presumably been fit and healthy enough to be adopted, so might well be still alive. But, of course, they had no clue by whom, or what his new name was.

'From my birth certificate, I found that my mother's name was Joyce M. Hetherington,' says Bev. 'So I applied for certificates of all the Joyce M. Hetheringtons born between 1920 and 1930. There was only one — Joyce Miranda Hetherington. There was no marriage certificate for her, but there was a certificate of her brother Peter, born two years after her. I also found his marriage and death certificates.

'His widow was still alive and Pam found out

she was still living at the address in Guisborough given on their marriage certificate. So I rang her up. I couldn't, of course, say that Joyce Hetherington was my mother, since she might never have told anyone she'd had a child, so I made up a story about a nurses' reunion. I said my mother had been a nurse and I was arranging a reunion of those who had worked with her, so I wanted to get Joyce's address. 'I don't know a Joyce,' said the woman. So that was a bit of a worry. 'But I know a Joy,' she then added. I replied that that must be her. 'I must have written her name down wrongly. She came originally from Guisborough, didn't she?' I asked. (I knew that was true.) 'I shouldn't do this,' said the woman, 'but you sound nice, so I'll give you her address.' Apparently Joy had been matron of Blandford Forum hospital in Dorset and was now living in Milton Abbas.'

Pam then acted as the intermediary, writing a carefully worded letter to Miss Joy Hetherington. They knew that she had never married, but, of course, there could be other people living with her who might read the letter so Pam was vague, explaining that she was trying to make contact with a Joy Hetherington on behalf of someone who had lost contact with her in 1947.

'She must have got a terrible shock,' says Bev. 'But she knew at once what it meant. All her life, she had told nobody about her children. She did nothing for about a week, then she went and confessed everything to her local vicar and asked him what she should do. He happened to know another vicar who had dealt with such cases and he rang Pam, to ask for more details.

'I wrote to my mother, sending some photographs of my children, and spoke to the vicar on the phone every night to see how my mother was feeling. I felt very guilty that I was causing her so much stress. At last she decided she wanted to meet me. 'It could be fun,' was the phrase she used.'

Bev and Geoff drove down to Dorset the next weekend, and in Milton Abbas Bev left her husband to look around the village while she went to see her mother.

'I was shaking in my shoes as I knocked at the front door. When my mother appeared, she didn't look at all as I had imagined. I thought she'd look like me, which of course was silly. She was seventy-one at the time and suffering from osteoporosis. She had already developed a hump and looked old and bent, though she had been five feet nine, much taller than me. I'm only five feet three.

'There was no embracing, no kissing. I just went in and apologised for having written to her out of the blue. I'd brought more photos of her grandchildren and great-grandson and she was thrilled to see them.

'The vicar was there for the first half an hour, but he left us alone when Geoff arrived. It had been arranged I'd stay for just one hour this first time, but in the end I was with her about three hours.

'I could easily see what agony I'd put her through. She had told nobody about having had twins. She'd shut it away, denied to herself it had ever happened, devoting her life to other people. The vicar was the first person she'd told.

'Since she'd retired, she'd become a recluse and gradually cut herself off from other people in the village. So it took a long time to get her confidence and trust. And even longer before the story began to come out. I didn't ask, I just waited for her to tell me in her own time. In fact it was four years before she even started to talk about what had happened in 1947.

'During that time, we went down to see her every five weeks or so, and gradually she came out of her shell. We went walking in the village and she began smiling and talking to people. 'If people ask who I am,' I said, 'I could be your niece.' This was to save her any embarrassment. 'No,' she replied. 'I must tell the truth.' So she started introducing me as her daughter.

'To her own amazement, everyone was delighted. No one thought less of her, it was the opposite if anything. All her life she had carried with her this Victorian sense of shame and humiliation, which she need never have felt. There was no stigma. Finally she could feel pride not shame about me and my family. People in the village used to say what a change there had been in her. They had never seen her smile before, never seen her so happy.'

Bev never quite got straight what had happened, back in 1947, nor did she ever find out the name of her real father. All her mother would say about him was that she had never loved him.

'On the very first day I met her, despite saying

185

she had forgotten all about us, she produced several photographs of Peter and myself in the pram and on a blanket, taken when we were about three months old.

'She told me she'd always believed that her twins were adopted together. That had been her hope and what she'd been led to believe by the adoption agency. But behind her back they'd adopted us separately.'

Pam believes they did this for the best of motives. They probably had a waiting-list of people wanting to adopt and decided to make two families happy instead of one.

Pam and Bev then began the search for Bev's missing twin brother, Peter. They could not get access to his court adoption papers to find out what his name had become, but Pam began to make enquiries through her friends and contacts at adoption agencies who had been active in the Bristol area in the 1940s, asking them to look in their files for twins adopted around the summer of 1947.

Peter's details were found quite quickly. They revealed he had been adopted by a Bristol couple called Joyce and Francis Townsend. His Christian name had not been changed and Bev wondered for a moment if he could be Peter Townshend from The Who, which would have been interesting. (They were of similar ages but, of course, their names were spelt differently.) She made a list of twenty Peter and P. Townsends in the Bristol phone directory and started working her way through them, saying she was trying to contact a long-lost friend whom she had not seen since 1947.

'On my eighteenth call, I got through to a house where a woman said yes, there was a Peter Townsend living there. I asked if he was aged about forty-seven, which was my age at the time. She said she thought so. Was his birthday in March? She didn't know, but it sounded familiar. Had his father's name been Francis? She didn't know that either, but she promised to pass on the questions and give him my name and number.'

Peter rang late that night while Bev was asleep. Her son took the call, but forgot to tell her until the next day.

'I rang him immediately,' says Bev. 'I didn't reveal much, in case he didn't know he'd been adopted. He had this very deep voice and was quite chatty. Eventually it came up in conversation that he did know he was adopted. He did not know, however, that he was a twin. 'I'm your twin sister,' I said to him. We talked for over an hour after that.'

Peter had been adopted before Bev, when he was seven months old. His father, Francis Townsend, and his wife had adopted a girl, Carol, four years before they adopted Peter.

'I didn't realise that I was adopted until I was about eleven,' says Peter. 'One day my mother mentioned it, almost in passing, when the subject came up in a conversation. I was astounded. She said she'd told me, ages before, when I was little, but I had no memory of it. I had a bit of a paddy, a little fit of pique, and a cry on my bed. Then I thought, it doesn't make

187

any difference, it doesn't really matter. So I just got on with life.'

Peter passed his eleven-plus exam and went to the local grammar school, but he failed his A levels and became an apprentice building services engineer. For the next twenty years or so he worked as a building services engineer for various firms. He got married and then divorced. He had no children and after his marriage he bought a house in Bristol, where he still lives.

In his spare time he became very keen on amateur dramatics, to the extent that he began to wonder whether he should have become an actor when he was younger. In his forties he applied for and got a place at the Bristol Old Vic Theatre School.

'I was amazed and thrilled to get in, but then the local council stopped giving grants. One friend lent me £1000, another £1500, and I set about raising the rest. I did two years at the Old Vic, which cost me £13,000. I should have paid back all my friends and supporters by the end of this year.'

Until Bev rang him, he'd never had any interest in meeting anyone from his birth family — for the usual reasons: 'I didn't think I had the right to disturb another person's life. And leaving it well alone was also out of respect for my adopted parents.'

Peter says his childhood was happy enough. He was well cared for, but he had little empathy with his father, whose job took him away from the family for a lot of the time. 'He had striven hard to achieve his position which for him was a

188

prime requisite in life. He was disappointed that I had no interest in emulating him. I felt I was often the source of arguments between him and my mother, who always took my side.

'They told me nothing about my birth mother — and I assumed they knew nothing, but funnily enough from when I was very little I used to have this fantasy, this recurring mystical scene in my head. I'm a baby being carried upstairs on someone's shoulder and I am looking back at rows of babies, as though I'm leaving a baby farm. I would have been too young to have remembered this. Perhaps I made it all up. But it was always so very clear.'

All the same, he never for one moment thought of trying to find out more about his background. If Bev had not rung him that day, he would never have done anything.

'But I was very intrigued when I got Bev's message. I didn't know what the hell it meant, why on earth she was ringing me, but I like a bit of a mystery in life. When she said to me, 'I'm your twin sister,' I said, 'Well hello, twin sister!' '

The first meeting between them took place a week or so after their phone conversation. It happened to be just before their mother's birthday.

'I'd arranged to go down for her birthday,' says Bev. 'When I gave her her present, I said, 'I've got another present for you — I've found Peter.' She said she had guessed this would happen.'

Peter and Bev first met at Bev's home in Kenilworth. On the way there, Peter talked to himself on a tape recorder, getting down all his

189

thoughts. He kept it running during their meeting.

'I just thought, this sort of thing is never going to happen to me again — meeting a twin sister I never knew I had. So I might as well record it. It runs to ten hours.'

Bev was struck straightaway by the similarities between them. 'Peter does look a little like me. I could see that from the beginning: same sort of hair, though he is much taller; same sense of humour.'

The week after returning from an acting job in Cornwall, Peter rung his adopted mother to arrange to see her, in order to reveal what had happened. Peter asked her first what she really knew about his birth family, to which she still replied, 'Nothing.'

'I then asked where she'd adopted me from. It turned out to be the Gloucester Diocesan Association for Moral Welfare, whose office was in Whiteladies Road in Bristol. I asked her to describe the office and she said it was downstairs in a basement. They'd picked me up from there as a baby and my father had carried me out on his shoulders. I told her about my childhood memory and she agreed I couldn't have remembered the scene as a baby, but said that she had taken me back there several times later on. Perhaps that's where I've got the image from.'

His mother was very interested to hear his news and seemed happy for Peter, but his father was not so pleased. He cursed the change in legislation which gave adopted people access to records, describing it as 'a can of worms'. He refused to meet Bev for another two years.

Over the years Peter and Bev made frequent trips to Dorset to see their mother Joy. They'd take Bev's children and grandchildren and they helped to care for her to the end. In 1999 she fell and broke her hip, by which time she was in the first stages of senile dementia. She died in the hospital where she had once been the matron. Bev and Geoff arranged the funeral and put a death notice in the local paper: 'Joy Hetherington, dearly loved mum of Peter and Bev.'

Peter never felt quite as close to his mother as Bev did. 'She met her first, and worked very hard to establish the relationship,' he explains. 'We'd all go down together to see her, and it was an idyllic place. Milton Abbas is like a Disney set, thatched roofs everywhere. Our mother's cottage was a very pretty old almshouse, but when she was on her own she'd just sit inside smoking endless cigarettes, with the windows closed.

'I was desperate to find out more about her, and her attitude to me and what had happened, but didn't feel I could upset the cosy inconsequential conversations she and Bev had. I usually ended up talking to Geoff on our visits.

'Once I asked her if she'd like to come and see me in a play at Swanage, just thirty minutes from her place. She hummed and hawed and clearly wasn't keen. She asked what time it started and when I told her, 7.30 p.m., she quickly said sorry, she couldn't come, she always went to bed at six. But perhaps I should have made more of an effort to get to know her better.'

'I still feel anger, stone cold anger, that we were split as twins,' says Bev. 'In my life as a teacher, I have taught scores of twins and I know how close they are, how much they help each other. I would have loved to have been brought up with Peter. That was my mother's wish, after all.

'But we did meet in the end. I love him so much. We have such fun together. We wander off and lose ourselves, singing silly pop songs together, laughing at the same stupid things.'

In 1994 they were invited to America to see Dr Thomas Bouchard, director of the Center for Twin and Adoption Research at the University of Minnesota. He was making a special study of twins who have been separated and later reunited. Pam had heard of his researches and had written to tell him about Bev and Peter.

'It was all terribly serious,' says Bev. 'So many tests and examinations, from our eye retinas to our hearts to our dental records. They checked our IQ: our sense of spatial awareness; our spelling. They gave us psychological tests — it went on for ever. Most of the time we just giggled. But it was an interesting experience.'

Bev and Peter don't in fact appear to have many physical attributes or features in common, but they are alike as personalities. 'When we were young,' Bev says, 'we both wanted most in life to act. I never made it, but Peter did, in the end.'

'It's been absolutely wonderful meeting Beverly,' says Peter. 'She is such a warm, bubbly person. Since meeting her, my life has been very

192

much richer. As a child I did feel a bit of a cuckoo in the nest, out of step with the values of my adopted parents. And Bev felt much the same. With Bev I feel completely in tune. I don't think it's necessarily a matter of blood. Though of course she is the first blood relative I have ever known — and the only one I have now. It's also that we happen to get on so well together.'

Pam Hodgkins followed the progress of the search and the subsequent relationship between the twins. And Bev admits that but for Pam, she would never have found Peter. So when Pam was contacted about a search for a missing triplet, she was very interested, hoping it could be as successful, and the emotional outcome as happy for the triplets as it had been for the twins.

21

NORCAP to the Rescue

Search was what the BBC liked to describe as an event, a concept, rather than just a run-of-the-mill, one-off programme. It was a major one-hour show fronted by Nick Ross and Fiona Bruce. Its subject was trying to reunite missing people, ranging from old school friends, to members of families who had disappeared, to comrades-in-arms who had once served together and then lost contact. The search need not necessarily be only for someone you once knew, it could be for someone you wanted to know more about. A man in Scotland had letters from an aunt written on *Titanic* notepaper and he wanted to find out something about her. A boy in Kent had been rescued from drowning in a castle moat and he wanted to say thank you to his unknown saviour.

Search was first broadcast in 1999, achieving impressive ratings. Over forty telephone operators had been employed, working twenty-four hours a day. The website had received 80,000 hits.

The BBC had decided to repeat the formula in the summer of 2000. By this time Gill had already appeared on local radio in the west country to talk about the Hodders' search for their missing triplet. Nick Handel, the producer of *Search*, had thus heard about the triplets' story, and wanted to feature them in his programme. But he had his concerns: 'Adoption is a very difficult and dangerous topic for television,' says Nick. 'You can get into awkward waters and be accused of meddling. So we did as we'd done previously when adoption stories came up — we consulted NORCAP to ask for their guidance and advice. As I remember it, NORCAP was not keen at first for us to proceed with this story, but I was none the less keen to use David and Gill in the final programme, being interviewed live by Nick Ross, in the hope that people would ring in with information on May.'

Pam's first thought on being told the triplets' story was that May, if she were still alive, might be anywhere in the world, and could still be unaware that she was adopted. She had come across many people adopted in the 1930s who had never been told, and that would certainly explain why May had never come forward. Such a revelation could have very hurtful consequences and Pam was anxious that a TV appeal might be overly insensitive and intrusive.

She contacted David and Gill to find out what they knew about May, which of course wasn't much. She discovered that they had never approached any professional bodies such as NORCAP, who would have explored all the existing records. She tried to obtain details from some of the adoption agencies who might have been involved with May's adoption. The National Children's Adoption Society, whose records are held by Westminster Council, had

May listed on their index, but their files had been destroyed during the Second World War.

Then Pam thought about their age. The triplets were now sixty-nine years old so the chances of anyone being hurt by events that had happened over sixty years previously were slim. Their age also meant that this could now be the last chance to bring them together. She could also sense David and Gill's emotional need to meet their long-lost triplet, and such desires and needs had been, of course, the foundation of NORCAP's work over the last eighteen years.

Pam was aware that this was an amazing story. If the reunion succeeded and turned out happily, it would make excellent ammunition for NORCAP's lobbying campaign on the government's new adoption bill. Adoption laws don't get changed very often. Pam and NORCAP had been lobbying the government as far back as 1991 when, under the Tory government, an adoption law review process began. In 1996 a bill had been drafted, but had never proceeded. But now finally the Labour government seemed keen on a new bill, especially after the 1999 Waterhouse report on abuse in children's homes. They wanted to improve and give extra funding to adoption, seeing it as a way of securing family life for children who would otherwise grow up in the care of a local authority. Pam did not intend to let this chance to influence the bill pass by either her or NORCAP.

But how could Pam get access to the missing adoption papers and find out who had adopted May? She knew that the Registrar General had details of the adoption, but they were not available to NORCAP or any other outside body. Only May herself, or whatever she might now be called, could apply for them, if she were alive, that is.

There was, however, one possible option. In the 1926 Adoption Act, a clause detailed that the Registrar General could be ordered by the High Court to disclose the link between a birth registration and an adoption registration. The clause remained in the 1976 Act. Section 50, paragraph 5, stated that adoption records of the Registrar General shall not be open to public inspection, 'except under an order of any of the following courts'. The courts listed began with the High Court. Where better to begin?

Case law had resulted in the Court of Appeal determining that the order should only be made in 'exceptional circumstances' and where there was potential benefit to the adopted person. Pam felt the circumstances were indeed special. The fact she was dealing with triplets probably made the case unique. She had certainly never heard of triplets being adopted before. It therefore made their case of national interest and importance. Secondly, there was the time factor, dictated by their age.

Pam had gone to the High Court once before in 1994, pleading a reasonable case. Her application then concerned a woman now living abroad who had discovered that her birth mother had had a baby boy before her own birth. The baby had been adopted. She now wanted to make contact with the brother she had never met. Her mother was dead, so there could be no upset for her. The main reason the woman wanted to establish this contact was that she had developed a rare lung disease, said to be genetic, which she wanted her brother to know about for his medical records. Pam therefore thought she had an excellent case.

NORCAP hired a barrister, who made submissions, and the case was won. They obtained access to the adoption records, but it proved difficult to track down the missing brother, as he had been adopted by a family called Brown. When they eventually found the right Brown, he was unaware that he had been adopted. He was initially shocked, but reunion with his birth sister brought him peace of mind and eventually much joy. However, it caused upset and emotional disruption amongst the family who had adopted him. The case, therefore, had been a victory for NORCAP in legal terms, but had not been a success in emotional terms for the family or for the organisation.

Two years later another adoption case had been taken to the High Court, though not this time by NORCAP. It concerned a birth mother who had given up her daughter for adoption and now wanted to contact her. Pam had been asked for advice on the case and she soon discovered that the mother had had contact with her daughter's adopted family up to the age of eighteen, when it had suddenly ceased. Pam therefore reckoned that the daughter must know who her mother was, or have enough information to track her down. Since she hadn't done so, it must be presumed that she didn't want to. Pam felt that this should be respected, and that the case should not be fought. She was worried that if it was lost, it would become case law, making it harder for future cases. The family had gone ahead anyway, however. They had lost.

Pam was convinced that the triplets had an excellent case. Although NORCAP could not afford to hire a lawyer Pam decided to go ahead all the same. She would go it alone on behalf of NORCAP, gathering her own evidence, mustering her own arguments and herself put the case to the High Court.

22

A Visit to the High Court

David and Gill were pleased that they had the support and help of NORCAP, and that someone so clearly strong-willed and professionally experienced as Pam should be dealing with their case. Pam advised them that they must each go to a local solicitor with various documents and sign various statements. Meanwhile she began to make her preparations.

The official letters Gill and David's solicitor wrote to Pam on behalf of their clients confirmed that they had seen their relevant birth and marriage certificates and that they were supporting the High Court application. The wording in each letter was almost the same, finishing: 'Mrs Temple/Mr Welburn, accepts that if the Court makes an Order to release the relevant information she/he only expects to make contact with her/his sister if she consents to such contact after a prior initial confidential approach by NORCAP. We hope this letter is sufficient to start a successful application.'

The letters had, of course, been drafted by Pam herself, to get the ball rolling.

'Then I went to the High Court in the Strand,' says Pam, 'walked through the front door and asked an usher which was the applications court. Most other people waiting in the queue for the court were lawyers, applying on behalf of wives who wanted to take out injunctions against violent husbands, that sort of thing.

'I was eventually called before Mr Justice Sumner. I told him I wanted to apply under section 50.5 of the 1976 Adoption Act for access to some adoption records. He asked if I had notified the Registrar General, and I said I had. (I had discovered last time the sort of things you have to do first, otherwise you just get sent away.)

'The judge consulted a few papers and books and finally announced he would adjourn the case for a week while the Registrar General would be asked to appear.

'A week later I turned up again, and this time there was an official from the Registrar General's office, whom I knew, waiting with me.

'The judge heard us both and at the end of our applications he asked if there was anything further we wished to add. There were some things I was still working on and he wanted to check some facts as well, so the case was adjourned again.'

In Pam's written application she set out her arguments over three pages, making seventeen points and enclosing copies of relevant documents and evidence. She gave her name as Pamela Hodgkins MBE, CQSW and her profession as a social worker employed in a voluntary capacity as a trustee of NORCAP, which she had founded. She mentioned that she had made an application to the court before, in 1994.

She went on to relate the basic story of the triplets — their birth, their respective lives apart, the reunion of David and Gill, their desire to be reunited with May, and her failure to get details of May from Westminster Council, which had led her to explore this final option and was the reason she was here.

She mentioned that *Search* was planning to feature David and Gill, which she worried might lead to some upset or embarrassment for May and any family she had, should they first hear this news in such a public manner. If Pam's application was successful, she assured the court she would make her approach personally and in private.

She listed the ways in which she considered the case to be exceptional. There was firstly the matter of them being triplets. In the 1930s, the chance of all three surviving was less than ten per cent. Secondly, under present practices, triplets would not be separated at birth, and if they were for some unusual reason, on-going contact between them would be maintained. Finally, she listed the possible benefits of a reunion to May. She may have lived for sixty-eight years believing she had no surviving birth family. Locating her would give her this valuable, even priceless knowledge.

The Registrar General's short, written reaction on 10 July 2000 to Pam's application was that the principles laid down in the 1997 case (the one dismissed by the High Court) should be adhered to: disclosure should only be ordered in 'truly exceptional circumstances where there is something more than the emotional desire of the birth relatives to obtain information, the wish to know, or the strong underlying curiosity to find out'.

Pam knew that she was going to have a fight on her hands to prove her case. She had noticed that the European Convention on Human Rights was coming into force in the UK on 5 October 2000 and she hoped she might somehow be able to use this, perhaps by suggesting that Gill and David were being denied their human rights. But all she did at this stage was to mention it in her next written submission to the judge, on 26 July 2000. In this submission she also enclosed some academic information on twins which she had come across, to supplement her argument that the case of the triplets was indeed unique. She sent a copy of an article from the *New Law Journal* of 13 November 1992, by Dr Elizabeth Bryan, medical director of the Multiple Births Foundation at Queen Charlotte's Hospital. It contained some fascinating facts and observations about twins and triplets. In 1990 7934 pairs of twins but only 201 sets of triplets had been born in England and Wales — one third of them identical, two thirds of them fraternal or non-identical. (The incidence of twins and triplets in England and Wales was similar to that of Europe and the USA, but amongst black people the incidence was higher, whilst amongst Chinese and Japanese populations, it was lower. No explanation was offered for this strange difference.) Dr Bryan pointed out that today all social services and adoption agencies try to keep adopted twins together, as Pam had mentioned earlier. From her own experience Dr Bryan was convinced that this preference for keeping twins together was right: 'It is well established that many single surviving twins whose twin dies at birth, or soon after, will grieve for their twin for the rest of their life, even though they have never consciously known them. Whether the intensity of these feelings derives from close pre-birth associations in the womb is not known for sure. What is certain is that the feelings are often immensely powerful.'

Dr Bryan observed that the 'special intensity of twins' relationships with each other and their frequent dependency on each other make complications for both the caring professions and lawyers'. It was an authoritative and impressive piece of professional evidence, which no doubt the learned judge read with interest.

Pam meanwhile continued investigating the effect the European Convention on Human Rights might or might not have on her case.

'I contacted several barristers and solicitors and asked their opinions,' she says. 'It took a while for anyone to come back to me, but I was playing delaying tactics by now. It was nearly September and I didn't want the case heard until after 5 October, when the new human rights law came in, in case it could help.

'The information I received was not clear one way or the other. No one could offer a positive, unequivocal opinion, so I decided to drop this angle for the moment.'

The judge wrote to Pam on 31 August, saying

From The Hon. Mr Justice Sumner

SEP 0 4 2000

ROYAL COURTS OF JUSTICE
STRAND, LONDON, WC2A 2LL

31 August 2000

Dear Ms Hodghins,

May Hodder

Since the application came before me on 14 July I have received further documents from both parties. It is right that each party should have an opportunity to see what has been submitted and to comment on it if they wish. I enclose copies of them. I also received a copy of a booklet, ACR110, on the Adoption Contact Register.

I have considered the figures kindly supplied by the Register General. I have not found them easy to interpret. With such large numbers on each Register it is not easy to see why there should have been so few matches. It could be that those prepared to hear from their adopted family rarely match those seeking to find adopted relatives. I find that suggestion too simple on first consideration.

On possible conclusion is that for some reason the Register is not working in practice as it was intended. I would be grateful for any comments or explanation.

I have also considered the valuable summary of applications. The cases of 21 December 1993 and 16 November 1994 are of interest. They were before the Court of Appeal decision in D v Registrar General but if more is known of the judgment in either case it would be of interest.

Finally I should mention that I have received from the Department of Health a booklet entitled 'Intermediary service for birth relatives-Practical Guidelines'. I have not read it yet but it may well express views relevant to this application. If either party wishes to comment on any matters raised there, they are of course free to do so.

I am content for any further views to be put in writing. If however any party thinks it more appropriate for there to be a further hearing, I should be grateful if they would contact my clerk so that this can be arranged.

Yours sincerely,

C Sumner

cc   Mr Kieron Mahony

he was now considering all the evidence that had been submitted to him by NORCAP and the Registrar General. He was sending each side copies, so they would know what the other had submitted.

Pam wrote back thanking him and pointing out again that there would have been no need for her to go to the High Court at all if the records of the Hodder triplets had not been destroyed during the war. She added that if the triplets had been accommodated by Barnardo's, as their older siblings had been, they would not be 'suffering the difficulties they currently endure . . . It may be considered exceptionally unfortunate for Mr Welburn and Mrs Temple that they too were not cared for by that charity.'

Over the winter of 2000 to 2001 written evidence continued to be submitted and considered by the judge. Pam admits she continued to deliberately try to slow things down: 'I was a bit Machiavellian, dragging my feet, but I had to do all the work for the court case in my spare time. I was also giving evidence in the House of Commons before the select committee on the new adoption bill.'

The judge made it known that he would be giving his judgement on 11 April 2001. On 6 April Pam sent by fax her final submissions to the court, apologising for the delay, saying she had been unwell for several weeks and also under pressure due to her professional employment which had left little time for her voluntary work on behalf of NORCAP members.

She brought up the subject of the Human

Rights Act just in case it might help her case, and she enclosed another academic opinion, this time from Professor Audrey Mullender, chair of social work at Warwick University. The professor wrote that in her opinion there should be a change in the law to give people the right 'to know their adopted relative's adopted name, as happens unproblematically in New Zealand and elsewhere. I consider that we are still faced with an urgent need to review the legislation that impedes birth relatives' opportunities to search and reunion.'

Mr Justice Sumner's final judgement covered thirteen pages. It started with a clear and concise résumé of the Hodder case so far and went on to describe the history of the law in relation to this case, and the various applications that had been made over the years. The judge did mention the human rights angle, but said it had not been considered in similar cases so far. He appeared most impressed by Professor Mullender's statement and by Dr Elizabeth Bryan's article, quoting extensively from both, in particular on the idea of the intensity of twins' relationships with each other.

In paragraph 34 he added his own comment: 'I assume that with triplets such feelings are just as intense. It may be more so as I note that there are forty times as many twins as triplets.'

By paragraph 35 he was getting near to revealing his decision: 'I have considered with care whether any harm or upset would be caused to Miss Hodder by a sensitive inquiry indicating that her triplets would like to be in touch. Mr

207

Welburn and Mrs Temple agree not to pursue their attempts to trace her should she decline any further approach. I see no likelihood of harm if she declines. I see considerable benefit if she accepts and meets her brother and sister.'

However, in the next paragraph he continued: 'But the question remains whether I should make such an order. I have given this matter much anxious consideration,' and he finally sums up: 'In the case of triplets seeking to find each other after more than sixty years, I am satisfied the court should make the order sought.'

Pam was thrilled by the outcome and the success of all the arguments she had mustered, the evidence she had gathered, the opinions she had sought and the way in which she had presented them, with no legal representation. One has also to be impressed by the thoroughness and care of Mr Justice Sumner — the Hon. Sir Christopher Sumner, KT, a judge of the High Court of Justice, Family Division — to give him his full title. His final thirteen-page report was clear and simple and relatively free of legalese.

From the point of view of Pam, David and Gill, perhaps the nicest, most heartening part in the judge's pronouncement was his final paragraph: 'Finally, I express a personal interest. I should be grateful to be informed in due course of the results of my order, whatsoever may happen. I am grateful for the assistance of Ms Hodgkins and the Registrar General.'

As Pam left the court, she cheekily asked the Registrar General's official, the head of marriages and adoptions, if he had the missing records of May Hodder in his briefcase, ready to give her. 'He said he might want to appeal. His office had two weeks in which to decide, so he couldn't let me have them until then.

'I rang David and Gill at once and told them the news, but I pointed out they must not get too excited, in case the Registrar General did appeal.'

In the event, he didn't. On 27 April he wrote to Pam with the information that had taken over sixty years to secure. It covered only three lines, but within these lines were the simple bare facts they needed so badly: who had adopted May Hodder in 1934. The Registrar General had also added a personal note in his own handwriting, echoing what the judge had said: 'I would be interested to learn the outcome.'

The outcome, so far, had been a marvellous triumph for Pam and NORCAP, which would prove of vital assistance to their political lobbying on the new bill. If, of course, there was a reunion. For all that Pam and the other triplets knew, May might be dead. If alive, she might be impossible to locate. If located, she might decide she wanted no contact with her siblings. And if that was the case, they would not be able to go any further. The judge had made it clear that everything must be done with mutual consent. Otherwise, end of search, end of story.

23

The Hunt for Helena

The search for Helena began on 28 April 2001, when Pam received the letter from the Registrar General giving her a few brief lines of information:

> Mr Justice Sumner has ordered the Registrar General to disclose such information as he may hold.

> May Hodder, born on 18 May 1932, was adopted on 1 May 1934, following an order made in Barnet county court and given the name Helena Mary Thomas. Her adoptive parents are Russell Eric Thomas and Jeanie Thomas of The Manse, 25 Ravenscroft Park, Barnet, Hertfordshire.

28 April was a Saturday, so Pam was at home with her family in Aylesbury when she received the official letter. There's normally little chance of contacting people in offices or using reference libraries on a Saturday. But such minor things do not deter Pam.

The use of the present tense in the letter, referring to Helena's adoptive parents, related, of course, to 1934. It didn't mean they were still alive. The letter didn't describe Mr Thomas as

Reverend Thomas, so in theory he might have been a layman who happened to live in a house called The Manse. But Pam immediately suspected he was a cleric. And the manse suggested he was part of the Church of Scotland or a Free Church, which made things harder for Pam. As she well knew, a Church of England cleric is relatively easy to trace through *Crockford's*, the Church of England's clerical directory.

She went off to her local reference library in Aylesbury and got out Methodist, Presbyterian and other clerical yearbooks, noting down numbers or addresses of secretaries of likely-sounding churches in the Barnet area. She then came home and started ringing them all, asking if any one of their churches had had a manse in the 1930s located in Ravenscroft Park.

After several calls she spoke to a woman who was secretary of the Wood Street United Reformed Church in Barnet and recognised the address though not the name Reverend Thomas. However, she said there were photos of previous ministers in her church vestry, so she would go and have a look. Pam waited patiently and a couple of hours later the lady rang back to say yes, a Reverend Thomas had lived in the parish.

Pam explained that she was a social worker who needed to contact him on a sensitive matter, but one that she thought would bring him joy. Where had he moved to after Barnet? Were he and his wife still alive? Did anyone local remember his daughter Helena and whether she'd had any brothers or sisters?

211

It was quite a lot of queries to be presented with out of the blue, but the woman said she would make some enquiries on Monday. In the meantime, Pam posted a letter to her with an SAE, going over her questions. The letter was on headed notepaper and was signed Pamela J. Hodgkins, MBE, Senior Social Work Manager. This is what journalists and researchers are trained to do: get your questions down on paper, confirm who you are, sound impressive but polite. Pam was a quick learner.

Sure enough, after the weekend the woman turned up an obituary of Reverend Thomas in a church yearbook. He was, as we know but Pam didn't, quite a distinguished Congregationalist and the author of two books of sermons, so his obituary was more than just a couple of lines. Pam persuaded the woman to fax it to her.

Meanwhile, at NORCAP's office in Wheatley Pam started searching their microfiches with two other NORCAP workers, each looking for relevant death, marriage and birth entries.

They turned up death entries for Russell Thomases who had died in Loughborough, in Cardigan in Wales and in Liverpool, each around the right time. But eventually they decided that Russell Eric Thomas who had died in Hackney in 1981 appeared to be the right one.

Pam was convinced Helena would have married and immediately started looking through ten years of marriages of anyone called Helena Thomas. (They considered that someone born in the 1930s would have got married between the ages of eighteen and twenty-eight.

For births later in the century they'd extend this.) The search turned up the marriages of several dozen, but one that had taken place in Chipping Norton seemed most likely to Pam, even though her colleagues thought it was too far from Barnet.

'I knew there used to be a large Methodist children's home there,' says Pam. 'It was just a hunch — that the daughter of a minister might go and work there. Call me a witch if you like, many people do!'

When they got the full details of this Helena Thomas, Pam was proved to be correct. Even better, she had married a Mr Minter, a more unusual name than Thomas, which happens to be one of the most common surnames in England and Wales. Having got their marriage details, they soon whizzed through the records and discovered Helena and Harry Minter had had three children, one of them a son called Stanley. It was fortunate they'd had a son since he would definitely still have the surname Minter.

'And I was pleased he was called Stanley,' Pam says. 'It's an uncommon Christian name these days.' Indeed they were able to find the correct Stanley Minter's marriage details quite quickly.

As well as births, marriages and deaths, NORCAP also has details in its offices of the electoral rolls, for which they pay quite a bit of money. So they moved on to looking for likely-sounding Stanley Minters. They found one living in Croydon, whom they thought sounded a possibility. Another search of Minters on the electoral rolls turned up a Helena Minter living at Dartford, not far away.

'When we looked at the roll to see who else lived in that house we found a Miss Thomas. That confirmed it, as far as I was concerned. She must be the other daughter or some relation of the Reverend Thomas. We'd found Helena.'

Only five days had elapsed since first getting Helena's name, which was pretty good going, even for the experts and great databases of NORCAP.

On Wednesday Pam rang Stanley Minter's house saying she was a social worker wanting information about Reverend Russell Thomas. Stanley's wife Sarah answered. She didn't know anything about Reverend Thomas, but passed Pam over to her husband. Stanley had to think for a moment, before remembering that Reverend Thomas had been his mother's father.

'I didn't want to mention his mother immediately,' says Pam. 'That's why I focused on Reverend Thomas. I knew he was dead, and it's less threatening to have a stranger inquiring out of the blue about someone who is dead than someone living. He might have been worried or suspicious if I'd immediately started asking about his mother.'

Stanley told her that Reverend Thomas was dead, which of course Pam knew, and that he had been a minister in Barnet. He could remember him, but not very well. If Pam liked he would talk to his mother, who would know more details. He would give her Pam's phone number and she might ring Pam herself.

Or, of course, she might not, which is what Pam feared as she waited by her phone that evening. But to her surprise and delight, Helena rang her that very evening. She sounded, according to Pam, intrigued and a bit confused, but not worried by whatever it was Pam might be inquiring about. Her father, after all, had lived a blameless life.

'I let her tell me about her father,' says Pam. 'I didn't use the word adoption until she did. I was still worried she might not know. Around thirty per cent of adopted people from her generation still don't. But she brought up the fact that her and her sister were both adopted.

'Then she added, 'and I'm one of triplets'. That did dumbfound me. I never for one moment thought she would know she was a triplet. I just couldn't believe someone who *did* know such a thing would not have bothered to track down their other triplets.'

Pam now told Helena who she was and the reason that she had wanted to speak to Helena. She told her the basic details about her other two triplets, and how they had been searching for her since 1976. She also gave her some brief details about the court action and NORCAP, all of which Helena seemed, unsurprisingly, to find very confusing. She asked if Helena would be willing to make some sort of contact with them and she agreed to.

The next day Pam wrote to Helena on NORCAP headed notepaper to go over what they had discussed on the phone: 'I am delighted that you are minded to agree to contact with

215

your triplet brother and sister.'

Under terms of the High Court judgement Helena had to officially agree to contact and Pam needed proof of this, otherwise nothing more could happen.

In this letter Pam also arranged to come down to meet Helena in Dartford with a colleague on the afternoon of 8 May. Beforehand she would be attending a morning session at the House of Commons where she would be giving evidence before the select committee on the Adoption and Children Bill. The two events might not be connected as far as Helena was concerned, but they were to Pam. One in a sense had been driving the other along.

If the triplets were willing, Pam wanted to organise a press conference after their initial reunion. She was convinced from her own personal experience and from her involvement in hundreds of similar cases that their meeting would turn out to be a joyous experience. That was what NORCAP had been formed to create. She wanted the world to share this. She also wanted the world to know about the work of NORCAP and their current struggles with the Adoption Bill.

24

The Second Great Reunion

Until Pam's telephone call, nothing had happened in Helena's life to make her change her mind about contacting her birth family. She was happy with her life in Kent with her sister Pamela and her children and grandchildren not far away.

Pamela had eventually found out something about her own birth parents, but not much. Her real name, so she discovered, had been Jane Tait. The family might have been Irish-Scottish or Jewish-Scottish, she couldn't quite be sure. What little she picked up did not inspire her to try to contact them and she had abandoned her investigations.

When Collette, Helena's daughter, gave birth to her own children, she became even keener about finding out the truth about her mother's background. She even told her that one day when Helena was dead, she would conduct her own search.

Helena would do nothing. She remained fearful of what she might find out: 'I'd had a very sheltered life and didn't want any shocks. I wanted the unknown to stay unknown, in case I didn't like it. There might have been health problems in my family, things which could be passed on which would be worrying. We've had enough with them already in my husband's family.'

When her father had been alive she worried that it might be disloyal to him to go looking for relations. Now he had died, but she had Pamela living with her. Perhaps at the back of her mind she also worried that actively searching out the other triplets might seem to Pamela like a desertion. These concerns had stopped her doing anything. And nothing or nobody had approached her, until at 9 a.m. on the morning of 2 May 2001 she had got the call from her youngest child, her son Stanley.

' 'Mum,' he told me. 'I've had the weirdest telephone conversation with some woman called Pam,' Helena remembers.

'From what he told me I thought it must be a church matter, something to do with my father and the Congregational church. It seemed a harmless enough subject, so after thinking about it all day, in the evening I rang the number Stanley had given me.

'Pam asked me what I knew about my early life. I asked her what she meant. At some point I mentioned that I'd been adopted. She said she knew that. Then she asked me if I knew that I was one of triplets. I said yes, I knew that.

'Then she said that my brother and sister had been trying to track me down for twenty-five years. When she said that, I started shaking like a jelly. I just couldn't control myself.'

On 8 May Pam visited Helena for the first time. She brought all the documents about the court case and explained the Hodder family story in full.

'I found Pam very sympathetic and understanding,' says Helena, 'although I was still very confused and shaky. She suggested that as it was my birthday, our birthday, coming up soon — on 18 May — I should send my brother and sister a birthday card, which I did.'

She also sent flowers to Gill. Knowing nothing about David, she couldn't think of what to send him. David and Gill sent Helena a birthday card, prompted by Pam, and Gill also sent her sister a little ornament of a horse.

'That was so nice of Gill. She couldn't have known I've always liked horses.'

They exchanged a few letters, giving basic details of their own families, and finally they spoke on the phone: 'I found Gill so much easier to talk to than David,' says Helena. 'It was strange how much Gill's voice sounded like mine. When they heard her on the phone other people in my family have thought the same.'

It was arranged that all three would meet up for the first time at NORCAP's offices in Oxfordshire on 29 June 2001. Pam asked if they would agree to a little press conference afterwards, once they had all met each other. They didn't quite take this in properly as all three were in a bit of a daze by this time, but they said yes.

Before the reunion, there was something of a family drama in Helena's household. She had been told by Pam that she should bring one person to the meeting. So she asked Stanley if he would accompany her. This did not please her daughter Collette. It was Collette, after all, who had always been fascinated by her mother being one of triplets, who had begged her to try to find the others.

'I was very upset,' says Collette. 'I wanted to come along. In fact I said all three of us should be there. I didn't think it was right that we were being dictated to. I don't know whether it was NORCAP's fault or my mother's for not insisting. I just didn't think it was being at all well handled.'

Helena therefore found herself in a difficult position, trying to keep her family happy, but she refused to alter the arrangement. She said Stanley had been involved from the beginning, as he had taken the first call from Pam Hodgkins, so she wanted to take him. They set off for Wheatley in a rather fraught condition.

David chose his daughter Elizabeth to accompany him. Margaret of course would have been in raptures and fascinated by this turn of events, had she been alive. David felt stabs of regret that she was missing out. Through Pam, the BBC had managed to get hold of David in advance and invited him and his daughter to come to London the day before and be interviewed on a morning TV show.

'They put us up at the Hilton Hotel, so that was handy,' says David. The BBC provided a car to drive David and Elizabeth to Wheatley after the show. They arrived at NORCAP's offices very early and had to sit around and wait for the others.

Gill and Jock had left Barnstaple at 7 a.m. in a mini-cab, hired at a cost of £210 for the round trip, and five hours later they were at Wheatley.

'As we went into NORCAP,' says Gill, 'some of the staff were standing outside the door and they took photographs of us as we went in. That was a bit of a surprise.'

They sat around for a while in a room apart from the press, waiting for Helena.

'I could suddenly hear people talking in another room,' says David, 'so I realised that Helena had arrived with her son.'

On her arrival, Helena's first reaction was the same as Gill's: 'Some of the staff took my photograph. I hadn't expected that. But Stanley had his camera with him, so he took their photographs. I wasn't too worried at that stage.'

After she'd got her breath back, Helena was led by Pam by the hand to meet Gill and David. The three of them were in the same room for the first time in almost sixty-nine years.

'We just had some idle chat at first,' says David. 'That's my memory. I don't think we talked much about ourselves, really. I noticed Gill and Helena were about the same height and that they both had small hands. But I couldn't say they looked like sisters. They'd never been identical, of course. I noticed Gill's hair was white while Helena's was a bit darker.'

'My first reaction,' says Gill, 'was, 'Oh my God, it's Kath.' Helena just looked like Kath, our older sister. I felt an instant bond with her. I just had to look at her to realise that I felt close to her.'

'The minute I saw Gill,' says Helena, 'I felt a bond between us. Much more than with David. I just knew right away — I belonged to Gill. It was a wonderful feeling.

'I can't say I noticed at the time much of a family resemblance. If anything, Gill looked a bit like my father's sister, my aunt Mary, to whom of course I wasn't related. As for David, I could see nothing of our family in him.'

After an hour on their own together they were joined by their respective partners. They were then brought a buffet lunch and some champagne while they still nattered away.

'Then Pam asked if we were ready for our big moment,' says Gill. 'I didn't realise what was coming. I had forgotten there might be a press reception. We were taken into this other room and to our amazement it was packed.'

Pam Hodgkins had in fact asked each of them about the idea of the press conference in advance and had got their agreement, though in the excitement of the reunion it had not registered properly. She herself had expected only one or two journalists to turn up and was surprised to see around forty people — television crews, and radio and newspaper reporters. One television cameraman told them that it was in fact his day off, but he'd requested to be on duty when he'd heard their story. He was fed up with covering nasty, unhappy events. He wanted a nice story for a change.

During the press conference, the reporters remarked on how the two sisters, Helena and Gill, appeared to be wearing the same white

222

blouse and the same sandals. Yet they had never met and didn't know what the other was going to wear.

Helena had not in fact noticed the connection until then, but she doesn't think it was particularly significant. They were not exactly the same blouses and sandals — they just looked similar. 'It was a hot day. Women of our age tend to wear the same sort of things on a hot day.

'I think I was probably asked most questions, as I was the one who had just been found. I did find it very tiring. I had never been interviewed in my life before. In fact I've only been mentioned in the newspapers once, and that was when Harry died. His inquest and the post-mortem were in the local papers.'

'I quite enjoyed the press conference,' says David. 'They asked me what it was like to meet up again, how did I feel, that sort of thing.'

'It was a bit nerve-racking,' says Gill, 'but we all survived.'

'One of the interviews we'd done,' recalls Helena, 'was with Radio Oxford. When we were driving home Stanley and I heard it on the car radio. It was strange to hear myself. I sounded posh!'

The interviews and attention on the triplets continued for some time afterwards, as the local media followed up the story, which had been in all the national newspapers. *The Times* devoted a whole page to it as well as an editorial comment.

On Sunday a BBC crew came to interview Helena at home, followed by BBC Radio Kent.

THREE CHEERS

For the parted triplets who have found each other again

Pythagoras considered three to be the perfect number, expressive of beginning, middle and end. It has remained evocative ever since. All sorts of things come in threes: from classical Fates to Christian Graces, from primary colours to clover leaves. The sundering of a trio seems particularly unsettling. So there will be many to empathise with the happiness of the triplets who, separated and given up for adoption at eight months old, have finally now at the age of 69 been reunited.

Their story makes a stock plot. From the fairy tale to modern fiction, the rediscovery of a long-lost family member has been a device to salvage happiness from misery and to restore harmony to turmoil. Siblings who share homes and rivalries might take issue. So might their parents. Who has never wished that another family member might be spirited away . . . and preferably vapourised in perpetuity?

Whoever has missed out on family life, is the answer. We so love to hate those copycat siblings, that even to be deprived of their irritations counts as a loss. Separated triplets would feel this more than most. Those who shared a womb, tend also to share a mysterious but enduringly powerful bond. Their mutual sense of identity, may (in the case of identical twins) be obvious superficially, but on a deeper level it is more profound. Lost twin syndrome, a nagging sense of incompleteness, is commonly recognised by counsellors.

Authorities nowadays do their utmost not to separate siblings put up for adoption. But in the 1930s, when these triplets were parted, each was given to a different family. That the two who first found each other in 1976 should, after a 25 year search, have ever traced the third without even knowing her name, seems a miracle like turning up the 'Queen in a three-card trick. The changes in law and more compassionate system which have made this reunion possible, can only be commended. And, though it is sad to contemplate the years of companionship they have missed, they have great pleasure ahead, looking into the mirrors of each other's life story, sharing every angle from their point of the triangle. The trio that was perfect at the beginning, was broken up in the middle. But poetic justice has been done. The account has balanced in the end.

The Times' editorial on the triplets' reunion

Then she did a link-up with Gill on BBC Radio Devon. On Thursday she went up to London, where she was joined by David and Gill for *This Morning with Richard and Judy* on ITV. They were all a bit disappointed when it turned out that Richard and Judy were not there that morning and they were interviewed by somebody else.

They also went on Gloria Hunniford's show. 'She was brilliant. She made us feel really at home. We all loved her,' says Helena.

Helena later did an interview for Radio Inverness. 'I was surprised they were interested, but they said it was a wonderful story. I was also in the *Kentish Times* and the *Sevenoaks*

Chronicle. Oh, it was non-stop. It was good and bad, really. It was nice to hear from so many friends from the past, people I used to know, who now contacted me because of all the coverage we'd had. One of the Sisters who worked in the children's home got in touch, which was nice. For several weeks, when I went to WI meetings, people were still telling me how they'd heard me on the local radio.'

The media coverage wasn't in fact all that intense. It just felt like it to the triplets, never having been in the papers or on radio or TV before. They were also fortunate that the reason for their fifteen minutes of fame was a happy one. Everyone rejoiced in their story. It was wholly uplifting with no skeletons in any cupboards. There could well have been unpleasant matters connected with their adoption — reasons why they had gone into care involving abuse, or worse. But the death of a mother in childbirth, while tragic, did not lead to unsavoury revelations.

After a while the requests for interviews and appearances began to die down, to their relief and the relief of their respective families.

Collette and her mother did not speak for a week after the press conference and the big reunion. The extensive media coverage, which of course surprised them all, made Collette even more sorry she hadn't been there: 'It was a bit hard to take, reading for the first time things about your own family in the newspapers.'

But they soon became friends again and Collette began to find the family reunion fascinating, and loved meeting all her new relations. However she admits she was pleased when it went a bit quieter. 'I wanted my mother to come back down to earth,' she told me. 'It has been a great upheaval in her life, especially at her age. She became very wrapped up in Gill and her new family. I still think she needs to calm down a bit.'

25

Sitting with the Standing Committee

Over the next year, while the triplets slowly got to know each other, Pam Hodgkins, triumphant from her High Court win, flushed by the success of the reunion and very pleased by the resulting publicity, bashed on with her main concern — the new Adoption and Children Bill.

On 21 November 2001 Pam had a rendezvous at Westminster to meet Angela Tanner, a social worker and the chair of NORCAP, who had come up from Bristol for the day to support Pam as she gave evidence before the standing committee. I was also there, to find out how the Bill was progressing.

Work leading to the new Bill had been going on for some ten years. New laws grind themselves out exceedingly slowly, especially when they concern children. The academic experts do their own grinding, sometimes with very small axes, as do social workers in the field. Numerous agencies and umbrella groups, each with their own points to make, their own corners to protect, are involved. Then, of course, the state has its own agenda, in this case one of their aims being to promote and expand the use of adoption generally.

In 1999 the Labour government published a large, glossy 168-page booklet called 'Adoption

Now'. It had been compiled by the Department of Health and contained the latest information and thinking, or research messages, as they like to call it, on adoption. In July 2000 the Cabinet Office published an equally handsome rather shorter volume entitled: 'Adoption — the Prime Minister's Review, Issued for Consultation'. Blair himself had written and signed the foreword: 'It is hard to overstate the importance of stable and loving family life for children. This is why I want more children to benefit from adoption.'

In December 2000 a white paper on adoption was unveiled by the Health Secretary, Alun Milburn, who described it as the biggest overhaul in adoption for twenty-five years. Its aim was 'to modernise adoption and put children at the heart of the adoption process'. Key measures included new national targets to increase the numbers of adoptions by forty per cent by 2004–5; the establishment of adoption registers for England and Wales; and £66 million to improve services and support for children and adoptive families, some of the money being specifically set aside for those who adopt.

In March 2001 the Bill was published and had its first reading in the House of Commons. It covered 78 pages and contained 113 clauses, plus explanatory notes of a further 56 pages. A lot of information for even the experts to digest and react to.

The general election of June 2001 brought the Labour government back into power and it was announced in the Queen's speech that adoption was still high on the agenda and would go through as soon as possible. In October 2001 a new bill was published and had its second reading in the House of Commons. Changes had been made in the Bill since publication, but as with all such bills at this stage, discussions and arguments were still going on and expert witnesses were being given a chance to air their views before a standing committee of MPs.

NORCAP was just one of dozens of interested organisations who had given both written and oral evidence and were now going to do so again.

When Pam arrived she was in a furious mood. Since the publication of the Bill there had been some changes concerning clauses about 'access to information about adopted children'. They were minor changes to most people, even to many professionals in the field, but to Pam and NORCAP they were absolutely vital.

Having won her two High Court cases and managed to get some adoption records opened up, she had expected that the Bill would make it easier for people affected by adoption to have access to their family records so that in future there would be no need to argue a 'special case' all the way to the High Court. After all, had not the judge agreed with Professor Mullender's opinion that there is an 'urgent need to review legislation that impedes birth relatives' opportunities for search and reunion'?

'It makes a nonsense of all the work I've done for the last twenty years. I might as well give up all my adoption work and open a tea shop instead,' she fumed. In a nutshell, said Pam, the changes meant they were now going backwards. Even the loophole whereby you could plead special circumstances had disappeared. 'None of us have realised that the new provisions will end adopted adults' unrestricted right to birth records information,' she told me.

Pam had expressed her disappointment in a written report that she had already handed the standing committee: 'We are utterly incredulous by the manner in which changes have been made and appalled by what is placed before you purporting to be an appropriate response for at least the next thirty years to the information of people affected by adoption.'

The standing committee was sitting, or should I say standing, in Portcullis House, which had been opened nine months before, having cost £234 million to build and been ridiculed by the press when its lavatories hadn't worked.

I was most impressed by the entrance doors — all glass — which gave splendid views from inside across the Thames to the London Eye. Inside was just as spectacular — like an indoor park about the size of Wembley stadium — containing not just an atrium, the sort you see in many modern hotels around the world, but an avenue of fully grown trees.

The public are allowed in to select and standing committee meetings, with no check on identities, but you have to go through airport-style security checks on your bags and possessions. Once through this, Pam and Angela spotted a huddle of adoption colleagues and chums. Some were waiting to go up to the committee room to give their evidence. Others had already done so and were immediately pounced upon and asked what sort of questions had been asked. It was like being back at school again and finding out what sort of mood the headmaster was in before going in to see him; or being tipped off who the bad guys were on an interview board. They named one MP who they said was dead bored, and they named the ones they thought mattered most.

We all went upstairs, along wood-panelled corridors from which we could look down and around at all the foliage and park benches below. The special standing committee on the Adoption and Children Bill was meeting in the Boothroyd Room, named after the former speaker. The door was closed and a policeman stood there, so we all waited obediently outside.

There was soon quite a large gathering of people, all from the adoption world, mostly women, who seemed to know each other. The age range, glancing round, was between forty and sixty. There was a good sprinkling of regional accents. I didn't overhear what one might call a posh or county accent. Several were muttering that they were dying for a fag, which reminded me of my late sister, Marion, a team leader in Camden for many years.

Five expert witnesses were to be called from five different adoption organisations, including Pam from NORCAP. Each had two or three assistants and colleagues clutching briefcases and documents. Then there were representatives from other agencies, keen to keep tabs on what was happening. As they laughed and gossiped and nudged each other, I could sense a certain rivalry between some of the groups and the different personalities.

'We all are in the 'adoption family',' admitted one of them, 'and like all families, there are some family members we don't like, some we don't talk to. But we do stick together when it matters.'

There was nudging and whispering when a gaggle of officials from the Department of Health arrived, the ones responsible for knocking the Bill into shape and ensuring that its wording was absolutely correct. Nobody I was with seemed very impressed by the depth of knowledge of some of the Ministry officials: 'You won't believe this, but when I mentioned the Houghton Report to — , he'd never heard of it.' Some of the officials were rubbished for their lack of first-hand experience of adoption, which of course these women had. But despite the gripes, the banter was good-humoured. I didn't manage to eavesdrop on the civil servants, but I expect they were muttering or thinking, 'Oh, no, there's that trouble-maker, don't look now or she'll drive you up the wall.'

The main door of the Boothroyd Room opened at 3.45 p.m. and we all trooped in. The twenty members of the committee — all MPs — entered in dribs and drabs from another door at the side. The room was dominated by a horseshoe-shaped table at which the MPs sat, with the chairman, David Hinchcliffe, the Labour MP for Wakefield, at the top end.

Opposite the other end of the horseshoe sat

the panel of five expert witnesses — four women and one man. Behind them was the public area where the supporters and colleagues of the witnesses sat, clutching their papers and factsheets, ready to slip them forward if required. Behind were several rows of unmarked chairs for around fifty members of the public. I counted twenty altogether, most of whom must presumably have been interested parties connected somehow with the various adoption agencies. At a side table, separated from both the MPs and the public, sat a small group of civil servants.

The chairman began by saying that if the division bell rang they would have to go off and vote, but they shouldn't be away more than ten minutes. Each committee member had a name badge in front of them, but not their party. You had to work that out, which wasn't too difficult with the help of stereotyping. The Tory MPs all seemed to be sitting together on the right speaking in loud voices and wearing blue shirts, neat ties and loud braces. The Labour MPs — half of them women — were on the left and had more regional accents.

There were no parliamentary stars or household names amongst them. The new Minister of State in the Department of Health, Jacqui Smith, was present but I didn't recognise her visually, only by her name. At the beginning, during the preliminaries, there was a bit of yawning from one or two MPs and a bit of giggling and gossiping from the women, but this soon disappeared when the witnesses were called. Each MP asked at least one question, but none showed the slightest sign of trying to score cheap party political points. One MP got a little carried away with his own importance, giving the experts the benefit of some rather pointless, irrelevant US statistics to show how much research he had been doing. Otherwise every MP spoke to the point and they were all utterly courteous, formal and polite while addressing the witnesses, trying to give each one a proper chance.

Most of the questions referred to specific clauses in the Bill on subjects such as inter-country adoption and rules for placement orders. Each expert witness was asked in turn for their views, which was fair but time-consuming since it soon became apparent that the experts did not have the same level of interest or concerns about all the clauses.

Each expert did in due course get a chance to ride their particular hobby horse, and so Pam managed to express her horror at the proposed changes to some of the wording of the Bill, explaining that it would be a step back of at least twenty-five years. 'If there had been no new bill,' the chairman asked her, 'would you have requested any of these new clauses?' 'No,' she replied. 'I would have stuck with the 1976 Act.'

She said she couldn't understand why the change to restrict adopted people's access to birth records had been made. The only thing she could suppose was that someone or somebody had made representations to the Department of Health. She would like to know, she said, what exactly these representations had consisted of.

Her question remained unanswered and there was some fidgeting from the civil servants' tables. The chairman moved the questioning on to other clauses, other witnesses.

At the end of the proceedings I had mixed feelings. The committee had been diligent and fair and appeared concerned to hear everyone's views, but it was impossible to work out how effective the expert witnesses had been and if any of them had got their real concerns across, made any meaningful points.

I'd also realised that NORCAP was just one of many interested parties in the field of adoption, and a relatively small one concerned about certain aspects of adoption law on which other bodies might have no views. The bigger agencies and organisations, such as Barnardo's, which has its own parliamentary adviser, had also been lobbying hard, submitting written evidence and appearing before the committee.

I later got a copy of Barnardo's briefing on the second reading of the Bill and they appeared to be supportive of it so far. The opening sentence of the document read: 'Barnardo's welcomes the Adoption and Children Bill as a key plank in the Government's programme to modernise the adoption system for the benefit of children.' But even Barnardo's had its reservations. The briefing went on to list their concerns, such as the proposed new adoption allowances (not one of NORCAP's major interests since their prime purpose was to support adults already affected by adoption).

When we had left Portcullis House I asked

Pam what she thought so far. She shrugged and said it had been no different to other occasions there. You did your best, took any chance when it came along and just hoped the MPs would listen to you. Like everyone else, she'd just have to wait and see what happened at the next stage.

26

Barnardo's Today

Barnardo's is what they call themselves today, usually followed by the zippy slogan: 'Giving Children Back Their Future'. The organisation still has its headquarters at Barkingside, where so much of its history, the history of child care and the history of the Hodder family began.

Today the main building is a brutal-looking, sixties-style concrete block. It's huge, but then Barnardo's today is a huge organisation, with 5000 full-time workers plus 250,000 volunteer workers. If Thomas Barnardo returned, he simply would not recognise it. The size of the organisation and the numbers of homes today would be the first major surprise for him. When Barnardo died in 1905 there were in all ninety-six homes with a total of 8500 children in their care. By the 1930s that number had increased to 188. But, as we have seen, after the Second World War society began to change. Social service departments of local authorities started to expand to take over the main burden of the problems of the poor and deprived, with local authorities creating their own homes and services. Gradually Barnardo's started to close down many of its bigger homes. In 1988 they dropped the Dr to become simply Barnardo's. Dr Barnardo would probably not have been pleased by that change. But he would have been stunned by what happened the following year: the last Barnardo's home was closed. So the answer to the question, how many Barnardo's homes are there today, is none.

Roger Singleton, chief executive of Barnardo's in 2003, has witnessed first-hand many of these dramatic changes. He joined Barnardo's in 1974, arriving just when the organisation was in a state of flux, and had to work out what their new role in childcare should be.

'The major decisions had been made in the late 60s, just before I joined. Officials had suggested that perhaps we should sell off our assets and go home. Our traditional function had gone. Once contraception had come along there were fewer illegitimate births and in turn the old-fashioned stigmas about single parents began to fade. People said we should respond to the new needs around us. Then Bill Cornish, one of our officials, put forward the idea of projects. He invented the whole concept.'

Roger found himself responsible for closing 120 homes: 'It was agony having to destroy structures and systems that had been going for almost a hundred years, but things had changed. In 1971 the Government identified 11,000 children in NHS institutions called mental handicap hospitals where children still slept thirty to a ward. Barnardo's played a leading part in closing them. Care in the community now existed to help such children. Many went to foster parents or to their own parents, if they could cope, with a bit of help.

'But at the same time it was exciting going into a new era and completely changing the concept of Barnardo's. In fact it's been thrilling creating all the projects over the past sixteen years.'

Derek Warren, Barnardo's communications manager, explained that there were three hundred projects in operation at present and it would take him an hour just to list them. He did outline one, which was fairly typical.

The project was in Wales and had been set up as a result of the well-documented scandal of children being abused by staff in several Welsh children's homes. The resulting investigations had highlighted the existence of teenage abusers in these homes. There were few services and little treatment or help available to them, so Barnardo's came forward to set up a centre in south Wales, which serves seven local authorities. Young abusers are sent there by the courts and social services. They have to attend for assessment, before being offered specialist counselling and treatment. The address of the centre is never given out, except to those who attend, for obvious reasons. The staff of ten — a project leader, two senior practitioners, five project workers and two administrative staff — are all employed by Barnardo's. They have a partnership contract with the local councils concerned for a set number of years at a set price and when the contract is finished, it might be renewed. If not, the staff will then move on to another project. Half the money is put up by the local social services and half by Barnardo's.

No two projects are identical. There can be short-term or long-term projects, with input from social services or collaboration with other charities or organisations. They range from helping teenage mothers to caring for young drug addicts.

★   ★   ★

One of the problems for Barnardo's nowadays is a lack of public awareness of their new role and purposes. They are still a household name, known by 98 per cent of the population, but most people still associate them with Victorian-style children's homes. To change this perception Barnardo's ran an expensive series of hard-hitting advertisements in 2001 in the national press. They showed gruesome adult-looking bodies wrecked by drugs, drink or abuse, and stated that the person had in fact died aged five years. It was reminiscent, in a way, of the shock photographs used by Dr Barnardo all those years ago. The message this time was that such people could have been rescued at a young age: 'At Barnardo's, we want to save children from a living death. Barnardo's works over the long term, helping 50,000 children a year who have nowhere else to turn.' In the small print, there was an appeal for donations, but money-gathering was not the major object. The aim was to correct the public's perception of the organisation.

Money is not in fact a major problem for Barnardo's. In 2001 their legacies totalled £23 million. That's new income, in one year, from people leaving or giving them money. Their total income, from all sources, came to £143 million. Some of this comes from their trading company, which sells things like Christmas calendars and has three hundred charity shops, but most of their income is from their accumulated legacies and investments over the decades. And they are rightly proud of the fact that 88p out of £1 they spend goes on their 'work with children'. (This figure does not include money spent running their charity shops.)

One of the departments housed at Barkingside contains the Barnardo's archives: 500,000 photographic images of every child who passed through Barnardo's between 1874 and 1989, when they closed their last home, as well as photographs of events and places in the history of Barnardo's. They also have three hundred films here, including two small newsreels taken at the funeral of Barnardo in 1905, now considered to be among the first newsreel films ever made.

The archives are hugely important, not just as a record of individuals, but of social history as well, reflecting things like changes in fashions over 125 years. Television producers, and magazine and book publishers are always asking to borrow images, but Barnardo's, like all organisations dealing with children, are wary about giving out material which might upset people still living.

On the day I visited, the archivist on duty got out some of their earliest photographs, starting

241

in 1874 with a boy called F. Bayes. His name and date of entry on the picture was handwritten, presumably by Dr Barnardo himself, who took all the early photographs. The photograph is still clear, sharp and, of course, heart-breaking, as was Barnardo's intention. Later photographs in the archives are numbered rather than named.

I was able to watch the 1905 film of Barnardo's funeral, at least a copy of it, as they don't want to wear out the original. It was more like a state funeral than a private one, with many carriages and huge crowds lining the road all the way through Barkingside to the gates of the Village Home.

★ ★ ★

Adoption is now a very minor part of Barnardo's work, but they do still arrange the adoption of around sixty children a year, acting as an adoption agency rather than a receiver of children. They also have a counselling service for those who were once in the care of Barnardo's and now want to make contact with their birth parents. Each year, they help to bring about many reunions of people separated by adoption like our triplets.

Ann Haigh, head of the counselling services, says that twenty years ago people were rather apologetic about wanting to trace relatives, worried that they were being disloyal to their adopted parents, giving lots of complicated reasons for their search by listing medical problems and family worries. But now people are aware of their rights, thanks to the 1976 Act and greater media publicity and are much less concerned about writing in for details.

If Barnardo's do hold the records, Ann will suggest a personal meeting with one of her staff to try to find out what searchers would like to achieve by tracing back their blood family. They usually want to meet their birth mother, or find out if they have any sisters or brothers, try to put the bits of the jigsaw of their life together. They are then given a written version of their own history which omits any information about third parties to whom they are not related. They can see their actual records, though they are difficult to understand, being full of codes and abbreviations: 'ad' stands for admission; 'bo' means boarded out; 'cl. sat' means clothing satisfactory; 'rmi' means routine medical inspection; 'ta' is tonsils and adenoids; 'md' is mentally deficient; and 'mf' stands for moral fall, which sounds most worrying.

It is pointed out at this first meeting that they might be taking on a long-term relationship should they find whoever they are searching for. This will no doubt be exciting, but may also be intense and very emotional, like a new love affair. Will they all be able to cope? The effects might be upsetting for their own family. Will their husband, or wife, or partner, or children be supportive all the way through?

After thinking through the implications, some people decide not to proceed any further at this stage. But many go ahead, and their missing mother or sibling is finally tracked down. At this

243

point someone from Barnardo's will write to them, not on Barnardo's headed notepaper — the address will simply be that of the counselling services. The letter will say something along the lines of, 'We are writing on behalf of X, who last had contact with you in 1970 and is now anxious to know how you are.' A telephone number is provided, along with times when a named person at the counselling services will be present to pass on further information.

Around half the birth mothers who reply are very pleased to have been contacted, having always wondered what had happened to their child but not dared to find out. Some are hesitant and want time to discuss the matter with their own family. Some want no contact whatsoever. But if contact is agreed on both sides, Barnardo's will then advise on what sort of letter should be written and where and how a first meeting should take place.

Some reunions peter out after the first few meetings, if people find they have little in common or don't actually like each other much. They can also become less frequent if one side becomes too dependent on the other. Others, as we have seen, provide both parties with a fulfilling, meaningful relationship.

There is also a syndrome that counselling experts describe as 'genetic sexual attraction'. Human beings often fall in love with people very like themselves and the attraction can be even stronger when they happen to be genetically similar, yet complete strangers. 'This attraction can be sudden, and very intense,' says Ann. 'These people are not locked into the normal incest taboos.'

So it can happen very rarely that an emotional reunion between a thirty-something woman and her teenage son leads to a sexual union. In one case it led to violent consequences, when a husband came home to find his wife in bed with her own long-lost son. Brothers and sisters have also been known to part from their wives or husbands to set up home together with the newly discovered relatives.

I did not of course expect such things to happen to the triplets, but I did wonder how Gill's husband Jock would feel after Gill and Helena's first emotional meeting, and, as the months went on, whether Helena's daughter Collette would be upset again, or if Helena's sister Pamela would begin to feel excluded in any way.

★ ★ ★

I finished my visit to Barnardo's by wandering around the estate, or what's left of it. Over the years, Barnardo's have sold off most of the original site, a lot of it to the local council for development. Where once 1500 Barnardo's girls lived in their Village Home there is now a council estate, a magistrate's court and a Tesco supermarket. The site of the Boys' Garden City is now a hotel.

To my surprise, one row of the original buildings from the Girl's Village Home is still

245

there, clustered round the last remaining of the three village greens, which comes alive several times a year when there are gatherings of Barnardo's old boys and girls there.

The houses are handsome, gabled-ended Victorian villas. Some are used today by Barnardo's as offices; one or two are lying empty. When they are renovated, they will be sold as private residences. They'll probably prove highly desirable, with such a sylvan setting.

At one time there was a high fence all round the estate to protect the girls, or to keep them in. The laundry, hospital, shops and swimming pool have gone, but the church is still standing, larger than I expected, big enough to serve a decent village, and in excellent condition. I went inside to find it bright and clean and very warm. The previous day a funeral service had been held for a well-loved Barnardo's official, a woman of fifty who had died suddenly after a heart attack. The pews were child-sized because, of course, the girls in the Village Home ranged from the age of two to sixteen. Money for the church was donated by one of Dr Barnardo's many wealthy, upper-class supporters, whose name has never been made public. In the entrance hall is a plaque which reads: 'In loving memory of her father and mother from their daughter. 26 June 1892'. So discreet and impersonal, leaving no clues for posterity.

In the corner of what's left of the estate, now overlooked by the backs of some modern houses, is Barnardo's memorial. It dates from 19 June 1908. Most mourners at that big funeral presumed his body was going to be buried here, but he had left private instructions that he wanted to be cremated, so only his ashes ended up on the memorial.

The monument is large, about twenty feet tall, and shows Barnardo with three young girls at his feet. They were modelled on three girls in the Village at the time. If you peer carefully you see one of them, whose name was Emily, has callipers on her legs. She lived to a good age, despite her disability, and married a local barber. The ashes of Syrie, Barnardo's wife, joined him in 1945. It was she who did so much to create the Girls' Village Home. Their daughter, also Syrie, was married twice: firstly to Henry Wellcome, the multi-millionaire, and then to Somerset Maugham. Despite the fact that he was homosexual, they had one child — a daughter.

Today, there is still a Dr Barnardo connected with Barnardo's: Dr David Barnardo, who became chairman of the organisation in March 2002. He is Thomas Barnardo's great-great nephew, a direct descendant of George Barnardo, one of Thomas's three full brothers.

He too went to medical school, but he actually did qualify, unlike Thomas. He eventually became a consultant in gastroenterology at Queen Mary's Hospital, Roehampton, from which he has now retired. He and his wife had three sons and then went on to adopt a girl and a boy.

'I have always been proud of Thomas,' says David. 'When I was at the London Hospital, I walked the East End streets knowing I was walking in his footsteps. I know he could be impatient and high-handed, and he thought the means justified the ends, but he was a great innovator in childcare and fundraising. Above his early homes hung a sign saying, 'No Destitute Child Turned Away', which was a bit over the top and probably not quite true. But just imagine anyone putting up a similar sign today over, say, a hospital: 'No One Needing a Hip Operation Turned Away'. Would anyone dare? Not likely.'

27

The Hodders Today

Florence Woolway, always known as Aunt Florrie, the younger sister of Kate Hodder and a bridesmaid at her wedding in 1919, was still alive in 2002, aged ninety-one. She had never married, devoting her life to looking after her various relations. In 1990 she sold her home in Harrow, bought a small flat in Sevenoaks and moved there with her niece, Evelyn Hodder, who had by then retired from her job with Hoover. Florrie had helped Evelyn through her various operations and with her searches for the triplets. Evelyn died in 1996, so she never witnessed the reunion of the triplets, much to Florrie's regret.

But Florrie herself has been involved in all the triplets' excitements. They have all been to see her, providing her with many relations she never knew she had, and lots of family news and chat. She insists on referring to David as John, his birth name, as she already had a David in her own family when he arrived. Her first impression on seeing him was that he was very like Wills Hodder.

Aunt Florrie is as bright as a button, her mind still very sharp. She looks after herself and does her own cooking and cleaning. When I went to visit her she insisted on making me a cooked meal — boiled potatoes with a ham salad, followed by apple tart. Her flat is very neat, filled with presents and knick-knacks given to her by Gill and Helena and other new members of her family. She had a stack of large-print Catherine Cookson books and some detective stories by Reginald Hill in her front room.

Living not far away in Sevenoaks is Pat Hodder — the last remaining of the six older Hodder children — the one with epilepsy who was not expected to live long. She comes to see her Aunt Florrie at least once a week, and does her shopping for her.

After Jean died in 1987 from stomach cancer, the three remaining Hodders — Ron, Joe and Pat — who had been living for many years in their grandfather's old house, the Post Office in Seal, decided to sell. They had been sitting tenants through three generations and had eventually managed to buy it at a reasonable price. They had then moved into town and bought a modern bungalow in Sevenoaks. It was there that Ron and Joe died in 1997, leaving Pat on her own.

I went with Pat one afternoon to visit St Lawrence church at Seal, where her parents were married. I drove and she told me where and when to turn, directing me precisely. She took me around the church and graveyard, telling me who was buried and where, and what the gravestones said, even though she herself can't read the inscriptions.

Seal is a very affluent, attractive rural community with no sign of suburban sprawl or modern developments. The church is very pretty and well cared for. You enter the gate through a wooden archway to the left after which there is a flat gravestone, which contains the bodies of Wills Hodder's parents: EPHRAIM HENRY HODDER PASSED AWAY, 20 JUNE 1955, AGED 86 it says on one side. On the other are the words AGNES JANE HODDER, DIED 12 MAY 1942, AGED 81. So she had been almost ten years older than her husband. On the Barnardo's document from 1934 recording the Hodder children's entry into care, I had half thought there might be a mistake in their ages: it said Ephraim was sixty-five and his wife was seventy-four. But her gravestone confirms this is correct. No wonder she could not contemplate taking in all nine of the Hodder children. Two was probably more than enough.

In the same grave are buried the four older Hodder children: JEAN PEGGY HODDER 12.7.1928 TO 13.10.1988; RONALD JAMES HODDER 28.9.1920 TO 29.1.1995; EVELYN EMILY HODDER 3.6.1922 TO 2.8.1996; ALBERT LESLIE HODDER 9.7.1925 TO 11.5.1997. (Albert went through life being known as Joe, but regained his proper name on his death.)

Behind the church, in a separate grave, are buried together Wills and Kate, the parents of the triplets: IN LOVING MEMORY OF OUR DEAR MOTHER KATE HODDER WHO DIED 7 MAY 1932 AND OUR DEAR FATHER WILLIAM JOHN HODDER WHO PASSED AWAY 14 APRIL 1963.

As we know from the birth certificates, the triplets were born on 18 May 1932. We also know that Kate died the next day, having given birth to them. Her grave, alas, has therefore got the date of her death wrong by twelve days. In her short life, so very many things did go wrong.

If she had died on 7 May, as her gravestone says, who knows if the unborn triplets would ever have been delivered. Certainly they would have had little chance of surviving. But she did give birth to them successfully, and miraculously they all survived the trauma of their birth and the dramas of their early years.

28

The Triplets Today

Gill and Jock still live in Barnstaple, in their bungalow on a hill just outside the town. Inside they have lots of ornaments, plus a couple of dogs and a parrot. When Jock retired from the Post Office he got a local job in a car park, which he did until he was seventy in 2001.

Their daughter Mandy lives not too far away in Somerset and is a care worker, looking after people with disabilities. She and her husband David have one daughter, Francie, now aged twenty-four, who is also a care worker. Jamie, Gill and Jock's adopted son, also lives locally. He married and has a daughter, Savana, now aged six, but the marriage collapsed.

In the year since the triplets' reunion, Gill has grown very close to Helena, who has been down to visit her several times. They write to one another regularly and talk on the phone every other evening.

'I did feel a bit sorry for Helena during the first few months with the media interest and all the new family relations to get to know,' says Gill. 'I found it hard enough twenty-five years ago, getting to know so many new people. It's a lot to take in, when you get to our age.

'I found the media attention more overwhelming than I expected. It seemed to go on for about three months. Hardly a day went by without a call from a women's magazine or a local radio station. I had enough in the end and started turning down things like *Kilroy*. David and Helena would ring me and ask if I was going to do certain programmes. When I said no they said they wouldn't either. It's funny they each asked me. It's because I'm the oldest I suppose — by three hours.

'I do wish for Helena's sake that we had found her twenty-five years ago, when I first made contact with David and all the Hodders. I would have loved her to have met Kath and Jean and the others. She's missed all that.

'As for me, I wish I'd met Helena when I was young. In fact I wish I'd known her all my life. It was such a shame we got separated as babies. I would have loved to have had her there during my teenage years. It would have been wonderful to have had a sister of exactly my own age — a best friend — to go through life with. I did have Raymond, but he was a boy ten years older than me, so it wasn't quite the same. Raymond and I are still close — I look upon him as a real brother. I feel closer to him than David, but that's not surprising. We have been through a lot together.'

Gill and Helena formed a strong bond quickly, as if desperate to make up for missing years. David would appear in some ways the odd one out, but then in all families some members are closer than others.

David still lives in Beverley, alone in the flat not far from the Minster that he bought with his late wife Margaret. Two of his children live not far away and he sees them and their families regularly.

'I'm so pleased by what's happened,' says his daughter Elizabeth. 'It's been so good for Dad, having all these new relations. I can see connections with all the Hodders. Aunt Evelyn was very touchy, lots of hugs, very like Gill and Helena. They are all so caring and Dad is the most unselfish man I know. He'd give you his last penny, go out of the way to help you with no benefit to himself.'

David realises that Gill and Helena have struck up a very close relationship and is pleased for them, without feeling at all left out. As a man, he is naturally the odd one out anyway, but he also has different interests and habits. He is still a strict Mormon and has not drunk alcohol, tea or coffee since 1964. Gill and Helena are both members of the Church of England, but fairly relaxed about their religious beliefs. They also like a drink or two. David is keen on long, early-morning walks; Gill and Helena try to avoid such things.

After the reunion with Helena they all went down to stay at Gill's for a couple of weeks.

'Gill and Helena stayed up until 2 or 3 a.m. most nights, nattering away,' says David. 'I always like to go to bed early, by 11 p.m., so I missed a lot of Helena's chat.

'But I got up at six one morning and asked Helena if she would like a walk. She agreed and it was good having a walk together, just the two of us. It was the first time I had had her to myself. I felt it was my turn to talk to her on our own. Oh, it was just chit-chat really, but I heard a bit more about her life story.

'Both of them kept calling me the 'pest' during those first two weeks — I always wanted them to come for a walk with me. I can't really sit still for long. No, I wasn't upset by it, it was just a family joke.'

David has been down to Kent to visit Helena and has met up with her in London, along with Pamela, her sister. They all went on the London Eye together and did a tour on a London open-top tourist bus. Helena, her daughter Collette and her family, and Pamela, have all been to see David in Beverley.

Helena is still in her house near Dartford in Kent, along with her sister Pamela and their cocker spaniel, Thumper. During the year after the reunion Gill worried that Pamela might feel a bit left out of Helena's new family, perhaps even resentful that Gill had come along out of the blue and taken up so much of Helena's time and thoughts and love. In some ways, Pamela did get neglected in the first few months, in the sense of being left behind while Helena went off on interviews, or to visit Gill, but she says she didn't resent it. She's been pleased that Helena has been so happy. 'I've pointed out to Pamela that she too could have got Pam Hodgkins to investigate her birth family,' says Helena, 'but she hasn't done so. I've always tried to include her in events, but she hasn't always wanted to come with me. Perhaps she is more of a loner than I am. I like to be with friends as much as possible.'

After the triplets' first holiday together in Devon visiting Gill, Helena went back on her own and had three weeks at Gill's house.

'I slept so well down there, better than I'd been sleeping at home. In those first few months there were just so many things going through my mind all the time keeping me awake. I'd think of all the new people I'd got to know, then I'd wonder about things I didn't understand, things I'd missed, people I hadn't got straight.'

Helena has also been to Sevenoaks on the Hodder family trail. She goes to the churchyard where her Hodder relations are all buried. 'By chance one day when I went into the church, the memorial book was open to commemorate the death of someone in the parish who had died on that exact day — and it turned out to be Albert Hodder. Wasn't that a remarkable coincidence?'

Everyone in Helena's family has remarked on her affection for Gill. 'With one or two members of my new family I've got to know, it has been a bit difficult now and again,' admits Helena. 'It's easy when you don't know all the history to say the wrong thing. It has been in a way like opening a can of worms, having so many new people and new relationships and histories to take in, but nothing awful has gone wrong so far.

'The more I get to know Gill, the more I like her. We can read each other's minds. We are just so close, it's unbelievable. I never thought it would be like this. All those fears I'd had for so many years proved to be groundless. If only I'd met her when I was younger. But at least we are now making up for all the lost years.

'I was thinking the other day, what if we'd all been girls, not two girls and a boy? When I came along twenty-five years later, would I have been able to get in? Would the first two have been so close that there would have been little room for me? It could have happened. So I'm lucky that David was not a girl.

'It is funny, all the cuddling I do with Gill. It's not like me at all. I have never been a very tactile person. But with Gill, it seems natural for me to sit and hold her hand.

'I feel I could tell Gill anything, anything in my head. I've told Pamela, my sister, a lot over the years, and I do love her dearly, but with Gill, it's different. She feels like me. She understands me completely. I don't want to be parted from her, not this time. I want to stay with her for always, laughing and crying together. I know that feeling will last as long as we are alive.'

Helena also worried during the year about the effects of her intense relationship with Gill on both Pamela and Collette. She senses they have felt a bit left out at times, perhaps even jealous in a way of all the excitement and involvement she has had.

There have been other little incidents of family tensions caused by the reunion during the year, mostly sparked off by Helena appearing to be carried away by her new family. 'But I'm thrilled by it all. The little upsets in the family are all minor really, compared with what I've gained. I get so much from Gill. Not just in love and affection — we've also helped each other a lot. The only problem is she lives so far away. I do wish she was nearer. My phone bill this last year has been enormous. I have thought it would be nice to move down to Devon . . . ' At this point Helena pauses slightly, lowering her voice. Both Pamela and Collette are with us, and a bit taken aback by this possibility.

'Not that I would,' adds Helena quickly. 'All my family is round here. So I'll stay here. Well, for the time being . . . '

★   ★   ★

In scientific terms, the case of triplets separated at such a young age and then brought together so many years later should be an interesting story. The Hodders are not identical, but they are still worth studying for the sake of the old battle, the old argument, nature versus nurture.

Pam sent off their details to Dr Thomas Bouchard at the University of Minnesota. She had previously told him about the twins, Beverly and Peter, and they went out for two weeks to be tested and observed by him. But Dr Bouchard replied to Pam saying he didn't need any more guinea pigs for research purposes. He had completed his current project, though at the time of writing he has not yet published his results. The world waits.

From my observations, I can't see many physical resemblances between the triplets. Helena could not at first see much connection between herself and Gill in appearance, but now that she has got to know all the members of Gill's family, she can see more family likenesses.

Other members of the Hodder family, on first seeing Helena, said she was very like Kath and Evelyn.

Some have said that David looks a bit like his father, Wills, and when he first met up with the Hodders many said he had a Hodder walk, like Wills or his uncle, Ron.

All three of the triplets have had a fairly uneventful medical history so far, but proper medical tests might show up more connections and similarities. David has always had problems with varicose veins and found, on first meeting the Hodders in 1975, that Ron, Joe and Kath had similar problems. Gill and Helena also suffer from the condition. Varicose veins have an hereditary element. Things like handwriting are mainly environmental. Helena has the neatest handwriting, judging by letters they have written to me, followed closely by Gill. David is some way behind. Helena of course had the advantage of an excellent private school and middle-class parents. David did poorly at his secondary school and never had to write in his working life.

Helena and Gill consider they are very alike in their personalities and interests, even if they don't look much alike physically. They both like embroidery and sewing and they were both presidents of their local Women's Institute. Over the year, they have discovered other more mundane similarities: 'Neither of us like puddings,' says Gill. 'We both prefer savoury food. We also laugh at the same things. Every time Helena comes to stay, all we seem to do is laugh. But I suppose the most important thing is that our minds seem to work in unison. We think as one person.'

All three triplets strike me as good people — God-loving, good-living, kind and generous. They have no apparent serious ailments, nor, surprisingly, have they had any serious operations in their adult lives. David would appear to be the fittest, not having touched alcohol, tea or coffee for over thirty years and still managing a walk of several hours every day.

David is still the odd one out, geographically and emotionally, and wishes that Gill, whose hospitality he has enjoyed for so long, would come and stay with him in Beverley. Helena has at least visited his home, though she has not stayed with him. But they do look upon him as their brother, love him as such and say they always will.

In May 2002 all three of them had a holiday together. It was a good holiday, happy times, so they all said. During their break, on 18 May, they celebrated their seventieth birthday. It was the first birthday they had celebrated all together since the day they were born in that Kentish workhouse on 18 May 1932, the day before their mother died.

29

Adoption in the Noughties

There were many heated arguments and proposals, debates and deputations from a wide range of interested bodies and lobby groups during the progress of the 2002 Adoption and Children Bill. There were also several delays, some caused by more urgent national events, such as emergency debates about sending British troops to Afghanistan.

Pam fought a long battle to change certain clauses as the Bill went through the Commons. There was some support for her changes, but not enough. In May 2002 the government's Bill was voted, unamended, through the Commons by 288 votes to 133. It made the front pages, but mainly because of a clause allowing unmarried couples, including homosexual couples, to adopt.

The new Bill proposed, amongst many other things, to give future birth parents contact rights with their children given over to adoption. But the government was unwilling to make any changes retrospectively, so Pam's struggle to give existing birth mothers, and birth brothers and sisters, the chance of access to their birth relatives, appeared to have failed.

The main object of the new Bill was to increase by forty per cent the number of new adoptions by the year 2004. So the concerns and worries of Pam and NORCAP and other agencies were by comparison fairly minor as far as the government was concerned.

In the minds of most people, it seems reasonable that the rights of the adopted child should always come first. As the one who has been adopted — given away — for whatever reason, by their birth mother, it should be up to them to decide if they want contact with her in later years. If not, they should be left alone. The birth mother, such people would argue, gave up her rights when her baby was adopted.

But this ignores the conditions of very different times between the two previous Adoption Acts in 1926 and 1976, when a woman giving birth out of wedlock suffered social, moral and economic pressures that often left her with little choice but to give her baby away. Such social stigmas have long disappeared. So doesn't the mother who gave birth during those times have some rights of her own?

At one time it was thought that regaining contact of any sort between adoptees and their birth parents was an issue in which well-adjusted, healthy adopted people wouldn't be interested. In 1949, this attitude was reflected in a government standing committee, which observed that 'provided that he has not grown up with the idea that his adoptive parents do not love him, or there is some mystery about his origins, he will not dwell unduly on these matters or attempt to get in touch with his natural parents'.

But since the 1970s attitudes have changed. 'No person should be cut off from his origins,' wrote Professor J. Triseliotis, Emeritus Professor at Edinburgh University, in his 1973 book *In Search of Origins: the Experience of Adopted People*: 'The self-perception of us all is partly based on what our parents and ancestors have been, going back many generations. Adoptees, too, wish to base themselves not only on their adoptive parents, but also on what their original parents and forebears have been, going back many generations.'

Today, adoption encourages not just openness but as much self-knowledge as possible. There is a fashion amongst social workers for what is called 'life story' work: an adopted child is helped to create and build up his own biography, with photographs and details of where he has come from, to give him his own genealogy and identity and thus, it is hoped, his own self-esteem.

If our triplets were being adopted today, or during the last twenty years, their father would have remained in touch and they would have known all about their other brothers and sisters. They would have enjoyed letters and phone calls with them, gone on visits to see them, and had their own little personal albums of their life and that of their birth family. There would have been no need to search or go to the High Court. But, like almost all adopted people of their generation, contact ceased.

In this age of increasing knowledge on how genes affect us and our health, it can be vital to know your genetic inheritance. During the summer of 2002 I heard a story of a woman from Dorset who had given up her baby son for adoption in 1966 and been unable to contact him since. She desperately wanted to now, in order to warn him that he had a fifty per cent chance of inheriting the gene for Huntington's disease, a degenerative disorder.

These sorts of stories, plus the arguments of Pam and others, might possibly have begun to influence the government as their Adoption Bill moved on to the House of Lords. It was there that a group of Liberal Democrat peers, with some cross-bench support, brought up again the subject of giving existing birth families some sort of access to adoption records.

In September 2002 Pam Hodgkins and Julia Feast of the Children's Society were suddenly invited to the Department of Health.

'It was so strange,' says Pam. 'It was clear straightaway that it was not going to be the usual adversarial meeting. Their attitude had suddenly totally changed. It was as if they were now saying, 'How can we help you, and how can you help us?' '

In October 2002 the government announced that they were going to introduce an amendment to the Bill during its final stages in the Lords. This new amendment would give existing birth relatives a statutory right of access to records through an intermediary service once an adopted child has reached the age of eighteen. The Bill, with the new amendment, was at long last passed and received the royal assent on 7 November 2002.

'I'm so happy,' said Pam. 'It's more than I ever dared hope we would achieve. An adopted child can still say it does not want any contact — and I'm happy with that — but it means that birth mothers and siblings now have the legal right to try and make contact. It's absolutely marvellous.'

The new rules are not expected to come into force until 2004 because there is a lot of administration to be organised, so it's hard at this stage to work out how many people might be affected.

During the first seventy years of legal adoption, from 1926 to 1997, over 850,000 adoption orders were made in England and Wales. Since 1976, when adopted adults got the right of access to their records, only nine per cent have come forward. Probably another twenty per cent have known enough to make contact unofficially. Factoring in say ten per cent who have died still leaves around 500,000 adopted children alive today who don't know where they came from, who their mother was.

Many of the mothers will, of course, have died by now, especially the pre-war ones, but if we assume that each went on to have another child, or already had one, then the chances are there are also 500,000 siblings out there like our triplets, with brothers and sisters, or half-brothers and half-sisters, of whom they are still totally unaware. Yet these are people they would perhaps like to know about and meet, to complete their own family story.

Now the law has changed, there will be many more family reunions in the future. But will they be happy ones? How often will they go wrong, and why?

Until relatively recently there has been very little published research on reunions between parents and the children they have given up. The biggest study yet of the subject began in 1997 when the Children's Society got funding from the Nuffield Foundation to interview almost five hundred adoptees and parents, the largest sample ever studied. Their results were published in 2000 in a book called *Adoption Search and Reunion*, edited by David Howe of the University of East Anglia and Julia Feast of the Children's Society.

They wanted to investigate why people search, what sort of people they were, and what happens after their search. They also studied the uninterested non-searchers.

Their sample groups were all much younger than our triplets, in their thirties and forties. Of the searchers, women clearly outnumbered men by two to one. In this case, our triplets were not typical. It was David, admittedly encouraged by his wife, who instigated the first search. Helena was a definite non-searcher. Gill was interested, but did nothing.

There were two main motivations given by the searchers for tracking down a birth relative: to satisfy a long-standing curiosity about their origins; and to fulfil a need to know more about themselves. The main reasons given for not searching echo much of what Helena had expressed: feeling that adoptive parents are real parents; not wishing to upset or be disloyal to adoptive parents; and fears of finding out information that may be unpleasant.

The results of reunions with birth families were in the main happy events. Over eighty per cent were pleased about the outcome. Even seventy per cent of non-searchers, the ones who had been contacted rather than gone out searching, were pleased with how things had turned out. These people had all experienced an improved sense of identity and well-being and also an extension to their family and social life. Around fourteen per cent felt the experience had been emotionally upsetting. Only six per cent wished they had not been informed about the interest of a birth relative.

They all reported excitement and elation during the first flush of their reunion, just like our triplets had done. Regular contact was kept up for the next two or three years, but after five years there was a marked decrease in contact and a large minority of adopted children, some forty per cent, had given up all contact with their birth mother. Siblings kept in contact for much longer.

On the whole, despite this eventual dropping-off in contact, there is no doubt that reunions are hugely successful. We must hope that the hundreds of thousands who now have a chance of reunion with their birth relatives will be equally happy and satisfied. It's a shame that it's taken so long for the law to change. A great many of those affected, the results of pre- and post-war adoptions like our triplets, are getting on in years.

'I don't expect another change in our adoption laws for twenty-five years now,' says Pam Hodgkins. 'If we hadn't won this time, that would have been it. It would have been the last chance for many thousands of people.'

Our triplets, of course, are convinced that they will stay friends and be in close contact for ever, for what's left of their lives, having been separated for so much of them. Helena, who never actively wanted contact re-established, has only one regret: 'I wish now that it had all happened much earlier.'

Appendices

A. Personal Survey of the Triplets Today

The triplets were born on 18 May 1932 and were adopted by very different families from different social classes in different parts of the country. At the age of seventy in May 2002, celebrating their first ever birthday together since they were born, I asked them to fill in a little survey about their personal details, habits and tastes. I wanted to see what connections there were between them, what similarities, if any, they had — despite being two girls and a boy, and not identical. Would nature or would nurture be the more important element?

DAVID was adopted by a grocer and his wife in Beverley, Yorkshire. He became a joiner on leaving school, then worked in an aircraft factory. Married with three children — two boys and a girl, one adopted. Now a widower, living alone in Beverley.

GILL was adopted by a divorced single mother who already had two children and ran a family guest house in Lynmouth, Devon. She became a dance teacher on leaving school, then ran her own guest house. Married with two children — one adopted. Still living in Barnstaple with her husband.

HELENA was adopted by a Congregational

minister, a Cambridge graduate, and was brought up in Barnet. She was sent to private school, then worked as a house mother in a children's home. Married with three children — two girls and a boy. Now widowed, living with her sister, also adopted, near Dartford, Kent.

	DAVID	GILL	HELENA
HEIGHT	Five feet and six inches	Five feet and two inches	Five feet and two inches
WEIGHT	Eleven stone and two pounds	Eleven stone	Twelve stone
RIGHT- OR LEFT-HANDED?	Right	Right	Right
OPERATIONS	Tonsils – aged seven	Tonsils – aged thirteen	None
ARTHRITIS	None	In one knee	None
VARICOSE VEINS	Yes	Yes	Yes
OTHER ILLNESSES	Eczema as a baby	Hiatus hernia	None
EYE COLOUR	Blue	Grey	Hazel
EYESIGHT	Spectacles since aged three – short-sighted	Spectacles since aged fifty – long-sighted	Spectacles since aged forty – long-sighted
HAIR – WHEN YOUNG – NOW	Fair Receding, grey	Fair Grey	Blonde Brown
TEETH	Top set false since aged thirty	Three missing, four fillings	Top set false
BLOOD PRESSURE	OK	OK	OK

	DAVID	GILL	HELENA
FAVOURITE FOOD	Yorkshire pudding, meat and vegetables	Roast meat, curry	Roast dinner
FOOD DISLIKES	Beetroot, garlic, mushrooms, shellfish	None	None
TEA, COFFEE	Don't drink either	Drink both, without sugar	Drink both, without sugar
ALCOHOL	None since 1964	Red or white wine twice a week; gin if Helena comes	Gin and tonic, white wine socially
CIGARETTES	No	No	No
FAVOURITE COLOUR	Blue	Pink	Blue
FAVOURITE MUSIC	None	'Time to say Goodbye'	Glenn Miller
FAVOURITE TV	Sports, soaps, mysteries	*Ready Steady Cook*, *Timewatch*, some soaps	Quiz programmes
TV DISLIKES	Sex and violence	Westerns, violence	Fighting and bad language
RADIO	Don't listen to much	Radio Devon	Radio 2
NEWSPAPERS	Don't bother	*North Devon Journal*, *Sun* on Saturday	*Daily Express*, *Daily Telegraph*

	DAVID	GILL	HELENA
BOOKS	Don't read books	Now and again	Read every day – last book was *Angels of Mercy* by Lyn Andrews
CLUBS, ORGANISATIONS	Church clubs	Local WI, ex-president	Local WI, ex-president
EXERCISE	A lot of long walks, dancing	Short walks, every day	Taking the dog over the field
CRAFTS, HOBBIES	None	Embroidery and sewing – forty hours a week	Embroidery and knitting – forty hours a week
HOLIDAYS	Twice a year in UK; twice abroad, to Australia and Turkey	Scotland or Ireland; twice abroad, to Austria and Holland	Scotland or Devon; abroad, to USA, Greece, Hong Kong, Singapore, Australia and Bali
RELIGION	Church of Latter-Day Saints (mormons), twice a week	Church of England, occasionally	Church of England, once a month
POLITICS	Not really interested, voted Labour at the last election	Not really interested, voted Liberal at the last election	Faintly interested, voted Labour at the last election

— What ordinary things give you most pleasure in life?

DAVID: I get my main pleasures from going to church. I also enjoy mixing with other people.

GILL: Watching the birds in the garden; meeting up with my friends each week.

HELENA: Spending time with the family; doing the garden.

— Do you play the Lottery — and what would you do if you won?

DAVID: I don't play it.

GILL: Yes I play it. If I won I would see that the youngsters in the family all had their mortgages paid off.

HELENA: Yes, I play it. I would share it with the family.

— Have you had a happy or just an averagely happy life?

DAVID: I have had a wonderful life, well looked after by my parents, with a wonderful happy marriage.

GILL: A happy life, with a few ups and downs.

HELENA: Very happy.

— Do you mind being seventy? Would you like to be twenty-one again?

DAVID: I don't mind being seventy. I've been fortunate. No, I don't think I'd like to be twenty-one again.

GILL: I don't mind being seventy, but I would love to be twenty-one again.

HELENA: No, and no.

— What are the best things about the other two triplets?

DAVID: I enjoy being in the company of both of them.

GILL: Having them as brother and sister.

HELENA: Gill and I have so many things in common like stitching and sewing that we can teach each other. David likes to take me for walks.

— What annoys you about the other two?

DAVID: I would love it if they would both come and stay at my place for a holiday. It's not happened with Gill in twenty-seven years. I hope Helena won't take that long.

GILL: Nothing, really.

HELENA: David does like to be touchy-feely all the time.

— Do you think you will always be friends?

DAVID: I don't intend losing them again.

GILL: Yes, yes, yes.

HELENA: Yes, yes, yes.

It's hard to draw many conclusions from the answers to my survey. Three English people aged seventy picked at random would probably turn out no differently. Their genetic connection as triplets seems faint, apart from the varicose veins. They are all right-handed, but then most people are. None voted Tory at the last election, which surprised me. They are all pretty healthy, having had no major operations, which is interesting, considering that in their very early life, they were not expected to live long.

B. Further Reading

THE HISTORY, LAWS AND PRACTICES OF ADOPTION: *Adoption: Essays in Social Policy, Law and Sociology*, Philip Bean (ed.), Tavistock Publications, 1984.

Academic essays by leading experts from Britain and the USA on various aspects of adoption, such as adoption laws and practice and transcultural adoptions.

The Character of Adoption, Mary Kathleen Benet, Cape, 1976.

A thoughtful study on some of the practices, problems, dilemmas and the history of adoption in the West and the East, past and present.

ADOPTEES' REUNIONS:
Adoption, Search and Reunion, David Howe and Julia Feast, The Children's Society, 2000.

A fascinating study based on the experiences of five hundred adoptees, looking at why some search for their natural parents and some don't. Includes figures and graphs, as well as authorial insights and wisdoms.

Preparing for Reunion, Julia Feast, Michael Marwood, Sue Seabrook and Elizabeth Webb, The Children's Society, 1998.

First-person case histories of adoptees and birth families who have been reunited, as well as advice in simple, straightforward terms, for those thinking about tracing their birth parents.

BIOGRAPHIES OF DR BARNARDO:

Barnardo, Dr Gillian Wagner, Weidenfeld & Nicolson, 1979.

Biography of Dr Barnardo, using material from the Barnardo archives. Mainly about his work rather than the man.

For the Sake of the Children: Inside Dr Barnardo's, June Rose, Hodder, 1987.

Also a biography of Dr Barnardo, covering much the same ground, but less academic.

FIRST-HAND ACCOUNTS OF BEING BROUGHT UP IN A DR BARNARDO'S HOME:

The Likes of Us, G. V. Holmes, Frederick Muller, 1948.

Rose-coloured memoirs of a girl's experiences in Barnardo's Girls' Village Home in the 1930s.

This Time Next Week, Leslie Thomas, Constable, 1964.

A boy's experiences during the last war in a Barnardo home. Leslie Thomas's first book, which set him off on a writing career. Not much on the Barnardo organisation, but some touching stories and good period detail.

C. Useful Addresses

Adoption UK: Manor Farm, Appletree Road, Chipping Warden, Banbury, Oxfordshire, OX17 1LH. Telephone: 08707 700 450.

Supports adoptive families before, during and after adoption.

Barnardo's: Tanners Lane, Barkingside, Ilford, Essex, IG6 1QG. Telephone: 020 8550 2688.

No longer 'Dr Barnardo's', and no longer with any homes, but an even bigger organisation today which runs at any one time around three hundred projects to do with the care and welfare of children.

British Agencies for Adoption and Fostering (BAAF): Skyline House, 200 Union Street, London, SE1 0LX. Telephone: 020 7593 2000.

Also has regional offices. An umbrella organisation and pressure group which publishes pamphlets about all aspects of adoption and a monthly newspaper with details and photographs of children available for adoption.

The Children's Society: 91 Queen's Road, Peckham, London, SE15 2EZ. Telephone: 020 7732 9089.

A voluntary society of the Church of England which offers post-adoption care and counselling for people adopted through The Children's Society; also does research projects.

National Organisation for Counselling Adoptees and Parents (NORCAP): 112 Church Road, Wheatley, Oxfordshire, OX33 1LU. Telephone: 01865 875 000.

A charity that helps adults affected by adoption, giving support and advice, and information and assistance for those searching for relatives separated by adoption. Also operates a register which may link those separated by adoption.

Post-Adoption Centre: 5 Torriano Mews, Torriano Avenue, London, NW5 2RZ. Telephone: 020 7284 0555.

A small, independent charity which gives advice and therapeutic support for parents and their adopted children.

Registrar General: Office for National Statistics, General Register Office, PO Box 2, Southport, Merseyside, PR8 2JD.

This is the address to contact for a copy of birth, death and marriage certificates.

Office for National Statistics, Adoption Section, Smedley Hydro, Trafalgar Road, Southport, Merseyside, PR8 2HH. Telephone: 0151 471 4313.

This is the address for adopted adults to contact who want a copy of their adoption certificate, or for people affected by adoption who want to trace relatives by putting their name on the government's official contact register.

We do hope that you have enjoyed reading this large print book.

Did you know that all of our titles are available for purchase?

We publish a wide range of high quality large print books including:
Romances, Mysteries, Classics
General Fiction
Non Fiction and Westerns

Special interest titles available in large print are:
The Little Oxford Dictionary
Music Book
Song Book
Hymn Book
Service Book

Also available from us courtesy of Oxford University Press:
Young Readers' Dictionary
(large print edition)
Young Readers' Thesaurus
(large print edition)

For further information or a free brochure, please contact us at:
Ulverscroft Large Print Books Ltd.,
The Green, Bradgate Road, Anstey,
Leicester, LE7 7FU, England.
Tel: **(00 44) 0116 236 4325**
Fax: **(00 44) 0116 234 0205**

Other titles published by
The House of Ulverscroft:

THE STORYTELLER'S DAUGHTER

Saira Shah

Saira Shah grew up in Britain, but she was always told she came from somewhere else: a fairytale land of orchards and gardens. The country was Afghanistan, the storyteller her father. Then, aged twenty-one, Saira set out to find the truth about her family's homeland. Instead of finding a paradise, she was plunged into a country at war. The journey spanned more than fifteen years. Whether extricating herself from an arranged marriage, walking through minefields with the mujahidin, or slipping clandestinely into the Taliban's Kabul, Saira learnt the bitter limits of the stories she loved. But she discovered the reality of a country more complex and challenging than anything she could have imagined.

KATE REMEMBERED

A. Scott Berg

For seven decades Katharine Hepburn reigned as an admired actress, a beloved movie star and a treasured icon of the modern American woman. She also remained one of the most private of all the public figures of her time. In 1982 — at the age of seventy-five — the four-time Academy Award winner opened her door to biographer A. Scott Berg — then thirty-three — and began a special friendship that endured to the end of her life. Over the next twenty years, Kate used their many hours together to reveal all that came to mind, often relecting on the people and episodes of her past, occasionally on the meaning of life. Here are the stories from those intimate conversations, and much more.